YALTA VICTIM

D1349591

YALTA
VICTIM

ZOE POLANSKA-PALMER

Introduction by
NICHOLAS BETHELL

MAINSTREAM
PUBLISHING

First published in 1986 by
MAINSTREAM PUBLISHING COMPANY (EDINBURGH) LTD.
7 Albany Street
Edinburgh EH1 3UG

ISBN 1 85158 001 8

Typeset in 11pt. Garamond by Pennart Typesetting (Edinburgh) Limited.
Printed in Great Britain by Billing & Sons, Worcester.

CONTENTS

ACKNOWLEDGEMENTS

My grateful thanks, as always, go to my husband for his tolerance and understanding during the writing of this book; to Lord Bethell who first recorded these historical facts in his book *The Last Secret*, and who has kindly consented to write the introduction to *Yalta Victim*; to Susan, who has played a special role; and to my publishers for their kindness and their infinite patience.

For my Mama and all the victims of political conflict.

INTRODUCTION

by

Nicholas Bethell

The nub of Zoe Polanska's amazing story is that she was both witness and victim of what was probably the cruellest and most treacherous act of policy carried out in Britain's name this century. It is a miracle that she survives and an even happier miracle that she is now able – after her experiences in southern Russia, Yugoslavia, Italy and in spite of the Austrian nightmare – to make her home among us 40 years later.

Zoe is a 'Lienz survivor' living in Scotland. It would be no more strange if she were an Auschwitz survivor living in Bavaria. The mental adjustment needed to make the transition demands a similarly high level of tolerance, understanding and forgiveness.

Ten years have passed since the story was told in *The Last Secret* and its resulting television film of tens of thousands of people from Russia – including old men, women and children – who were tricked, beaten and bayoneted onto cattle trucks, a few days after the war was won in 1945, so that Stalin could execute some of them (the lucky ones) and starve or freeze the rest to death or decrepitude.

It is five years since Zoe, the story's most touching character in both book and film, dedicated the memorial to the innocent victims of the Yalta Agreement, the memorial in central London that was almost immediately and very sophistically vandalised, presumably by the Soviet Union's supporters, and awaits reconstruction. Many people who read Zoe's words or saw her on the screen have wondered who she is and how she ever came to that terrible place in Austria where so many were killed. Now they have a book that gives them a chance to find out.

The Scottish soldiers who carried out the operation, just outside the small town of Lienz, were told simply that it was their job to deal with war criminals and traitors to the 'glorious Soviet ally'. They had fought their way up through Italy and were glad to be alive after nearly six years of war. They had no reason to be sympathetic towards men who had joined Hitler's Germany and fought against their own country.

Yet even they, the legendarily tough 'Jocks' of the Argyll and Sutherland Highlanders, were disgusted by what they had to do, to the point of near mutiny. They had got to know their Russian prisoners, most of them from the Cossack community, and they found themselves unable to share the official view, repeated by Harold Macmillan in a recent television interview, that these people were all 'no more than barbarians'.

It became clear that these extraordinary people, with their 'Wild West' caravans and horses that seemed to fly, were men who had good reason to be the Soviet Union's enemies. Their families had been slaughtered by Lenin's and Stalin's secret police, their land taken away so that they starved. They were wives and small children who had retreated from Russia with their menfolk. Some of the men, it is true, had fought cruelly under German command. Others were innocent. The trouble is that in Lienz in May/June 1945 there was no British authority ready to make the distinction between the two.

They were teenage boys and girls who had taken no part in the war, who had merely been caught up in the general chaos of the German occupation and Soviet reconquest of eastern Europe. One of these was Zoe Polanska, a child on the edge of womanhood, innocent of any offence, certainly not a barbarian.

The British Cabinet's decision of September 1944 was that British soldiers must return all Soviet citizens, even children like Zoe, to the authorities of the Soviet Union, to whom they 'belonged'. Mr Macmillan, now Lord Stockton, was part of that government. He has yet to explain why they did it.

They actually put her on the train to Austria's eastern zone. If that train had started a few minutes earlier, if one kindly officer had not taken her off, handed her over to his medical team and made sure they looked after the injuries she had received in the mêlée, she would certainly have vanished into the archipelago of Stalin's labour camps and probably never lived to tell the tale, let alone succeed in submitting the tale to a Scottish publisher.

Fortunately, as everyone who meets her will tell you, Zoe is very much alive. And so is the book which follows.

CHAPTER ONE

IN SEARCH OF A PAST

It was a spring day in March 1961. I picked up the telephone and dialled the number given in the small advertisement in my local newspaper. After what seemed like an interminable pause I was put through to the director who was dealing with the Moscow Trades Fair.

All trace of any confidence I had managed to muster disappeared as a deep husky voice, at once both severe and impatient, began firing questions at me.

'Have you any experience in the Trades? Do you speak Russian well?'

'Yes . . . I was born in Russia,' I managed to get my reply in.

There was a brief silence. I began to feel hot and became conscious of the little beads of sweat gathering on my forehead. His unfriendly voice was not encouraging, but I forced myself to listen on.

'Do you know anything about aprons, rollers or textile machinery?'

I explained naïvely that I thought one used aprons in the kitchen.

'No, no, no.' His words exploded into strong guffaws of laughter. 'You had better come and see me tomorrow before we close and I'll show you round the factory.'

That night, as my husband Arthur was on night duty, I was alone in the house. My fitful sleep was punctuated with nightmares: ghosts from the past gnawed at my subconscious.

The dawn brought a big day for me. I was to meet this unfriendly man who, unknown to him, held the power to give me a new hope for my venture. I made myself presentable and arrived punctually at the Dayco for my appointment. Twenty minutes later, I was taken to an office where I found a large-framed man, almost completely bald except for a few tufts of hair sticking out from the sides of his head. He was slightly bent over a highly polished desk, fumbling with a mass of papers.

'Ah, you must be Zoe. How do you do.' Dougal Gold glanced up from under his dark-framed glasses, looking straight at me and revealing his soft, bright blue eyes. It was then that I detected a

15

faint hope of kindness underlying the stern exterior.

He explained that his company, which manufactured textile machinery and accessories, was needing an interpreter for their visit to the first British Trades Fair in Moscow in two months time. I now think that he must have been only too glad to find a native Russian speaker on his doorstep. I had hardly told him about myself before I learned that the position was mine if I wanted it.

Tentatively, I broached the subject of contacting my parents: my only reason for wanting the job.

'No problem. We can manage without you for a couple of days. Go ahead and let them know you'll be in Moscow,' he replied without a moment's hesitation. This generosity was to prove a much deeper insight into his character than my initial, disembodied, impression.

The first hurdle had been crossed quickly and painlessly. But the weeks that followed were to be filled with emotional turmoil and bureaucratic wrangling.

Eighteen years had passed since I had been dragged away from my home in Russia by the Nazi soldiers. In all those years I had never given up hope of returning to see my family. The thought that Stalin's reign of terror had now ended gave me little or no comfort. I knew myself that I had done no wrong, but had no way of knowing whether the Soviet government would see it that way. I lived in the West and had married a foreigner. Therefore I had betrayed my homeland.

Dayco were refused a visa on my behalf so I sought the advice of the British Foreign Office. Their reply spelt out my position only too clearly:

... it is understood that neither your marriage in 1948 nor your consequent acquisition of British nationality will have caused you to lose Soviet citizenship, which it is assumed you possessed ...

If you visit the Soviet Union while a Soviet citizen, the authorities of the Soviet Union will be entitled to treat you in the same way as a person who has only Soviet citizenship, and it is possible that you will not be able to obtain permission to leave the Soviet Union again even if you enter that country with a Soviet entry-exit visa in your United Kingdom passport. You should understand that, as long as you possess Soviet citizenship, the British Embassy in Moscow will have no standing to make official representation on your behalf.

To make matters worse, the Russian Embassy in London informed me that if I wished to apply to be released from my Soviet citizenship I would have to present myself at the Supreme Court in Moscow. If this were refused then I may not be able to leave the country, but if granted then I certainly would not be able to visit my parents.

My husband and I endlessly discussed the risks involved, but there was only ever one choice I could make. I decided to follow my instinct and the slim chance that I would be able to see Mama again, and prepared myself to face any consequence.

The time before my departure was spent at my local library brushing up on my technical Russian language and, with the Dayco, acquainting myself with their products and helping to arrange the trip.

Shortly before I left I took a long walk, alone with my thoughts, not sure whether this was my last night in Scotland. A chilly breeze blew through the darkness from the River Tay. I stood by Broughty Ferry Castle, and closed my eyes.

Deeply wounding memories crowded my thoughts, together with new fears – for the month ahead of me. I could not pretend that I was not worried about my trip to Moscow and about all the sinister stories I had read of mysterious disappearances. Could it happen to me? Had I not already brushed with the KGB in the 'safety' of my own home?

Not long after our arrival in Angus, Scotland, one of my letters to Mama had been intercepted, and brought to me at our cottage by two Soviet agents. They had been reluctant to let Arthur take their coats to hang in the hall. I remember his horror when he realised why – a revolver had dropped out of one of the pockets.

They did not like the way I was living and questioned my choice to stay in the West when I had a family and a home in Russia. They were unaware that I had witnessed the Forcible Repatriation at Lienz. I knew the fate of those who returned. Would I not like a job at the Soviet Embassy in London and a free passage to Russia? My husband could follow me later. I declined the offer and they never returned

*

Who was to know what might happen in Moscow? Hot tears of

frustration started trickling down my cheeks. I was frightened and lonely.

16 May, 1961. It was the warmest day in London. The sun was hot enough for me to wear the white summer coat with matching shoes and the pale blue dress which I had bought specially for my trip.

My hands were stiff as I carried my hand luggage at Heathrow Airport. I could hardly count all the different types of aircraft waiting on the runways and whistling past the passenger buildings. Five of us were travelling together from my company. There was no direct flight to Moscow, so we were to fly first to Amsterdam.

I placed myself at the back of what seemed to me a very imposing plane and kept myself busy taking notes about our daily schedule for the exhibition. This was my first journey by air and it was an unnerving experience, being suspended high in the sky among the clouds. It seemed a world distant from the way I made my journey all those years ago.

My fellow passengers came from all walks of life. I listened to their conversations: the factory owners, drapers, industrialists, all ambitious to secure export orders within the Soviet Union.

As the plane flew closer to the city of Amsterdam acres of flower fields came into view, the different shades of blooms sparkling like diamonds in the sun. The landing on the glossy runway was perfect.

I was overawed by all the bustle and excitement as we approached the passenger terminal. Suddenly, I thought I heard my name announced on the Tannoy. It *was* my name – I was to report to the Customs Office. I exchanged looks with Mr Gold; was my journey going to end even before it had really started? When I reached the Customs Office, not without some trepidation, I scarcely had time to recognise the good-looking man waiting there before he flung his arms around me, winking as he whispered, 'I am your long-lost cousin, remember?'

My 'long-lost cousin' was in fact a friend whom I had last seen at a wedding in Scotland some years earlier. He had heard of my anxiety about my trip to Moscow and that I was to change flights in Amsterdam, where he was living. Standing patiently by Benny was a tall young woman, her eyes sparkling with a message of peace. We sat in the office and chatted for twenty minutes or so, surrounded by so many pots of tulips and daffodils that it seemed like we were back at the wedding reception.

IN SEARCH OF A PAST

I learned that the young woman was a friend of Benny's who also lived in Amsterdam. Her life and mine had followed parallel paths across war-torn Europe, only she had eventually married a Dutchman where I had settled in Britain. More important to me, she told me that she had recently returned from an untroubled holiday in Odessa, where she had been reunited with her family, free from any interference from the Soviet government. The reassurance gave me new courage and Benny was able to telephone my husband in Scotland and let him know that I had resumed my journey with a lighter heart.

I was humbly moved by my friend's thoughtfulness and have blessed him many times since.

*

I fell asleep almost as soon as the new plane took off, and woke up to find that we were flying among the grey clouds over Soviet territory. We continued for two hours over endless miles of dark-brown earth and green plains, scattered with clusters of trees and buildings. As the weather began to brighten I eagerly craned my neck to have a closer look at the countryside, anxious not to miss anything. Our journey took us over Copenhagen, Riga and Welikys Luki – I still have the flight plan which was passed round the aircraft. It was about ten thirty in the evening, local time, when we landed at Moscow International Airport, only a few minutes late.

I'm not sure what I had expected to find, but Moscow Airport was much the same as our earlier ports of call. Noisy, colourful and teeming with passengers, many of them British.

Mr Gold found us a taxi to take us along the bumpy road from the outskirts of Moscow to our hotel. As they wandered near the road, the white and brown cows looked well fed in the green fields. They lifted their heads now and then, as though to greet the newcomers. We drove further into the city and every building, new and old, seemed to glow with warmth. Some of the houses appeared to be in need of repair, but the gardens were neatly laid out. All the streets were laden with cherry trees in full blossom. I could see no graffiti, or litter on the streets.

The Ostankino hotel, an old and imposing building, was to be our base for the month's duration of the exhibition. It had certain strict rules, though I was never sure what they all were. No other person was to enter my room, for instance; even Mr Gold had to

19

use the telephone, never a personal communication.

The *zavedovna* (a kind of female concierge) made sure that all such rules were adhered to. She seemed to be everywhere at once! A middle-aged woman, dressed in a black skirt and white blouse, she had blue eyes deeply set into a pale, tired face and wore a little lipstick on her narrow lips. I found it odd that this woman carried out not only domestic work, but all sorts of repairs, including the plumbing.

In the evenings she would sit on an old sofa in a corner of the corridor, a woollen jacket drawn over her shoulders. She had to enter all the night activities into her report book. There were many such activities, not all involving the tourists!

One day, after we had been in Moscow for a while, I returned to my room unexpectedly. As I turned the corner in the corridor I saw a man leaving my room. Inside, I found that my suitcase had been forced open and the film exposed from my camera. My photographs had been personal — and very precious — but I was never to see them. That unpleasant incident makes me angry even now, but there seemed to be nothing I could do and no one to complain to.

*

Once I had settled into the hotel I began my attempt to contact my family. It was uncertain whether my letters informing them of my impending visit had reached their destination. No reply had arrived before I left Scotland. Our correspondence had been difficult over the years and I had learned not to rely on the arrival of any letter, however harmless the contents might be. All attempts to bring Mama to the West for a visit had been blocked; I did not expect much co-operation from the government now that I had decided to visit her.

My family lived many miles from Moscow, in the Odessa region of the Ukraine. There was nowhere I knew of where I could telephone them, or even leave a message. I had brushed aside these practicalities when planning my venture, with the optimism of one who had learned to face each problem as it arose. I think that I must have blindly clung to the hope that Mama would be waiting for me when I stepped off the plane at Moscow Airport.

It was not to be so easy. When I turned to the British Embassy for advice I was coldly informed that there was no chance whatsoever that the Soviet government would issue me with a permit to travel to the Odessa region. There was not enough time for the paperwork to go through; the travel arrangements would be too complicated; and, no, there was no point in trying to phone again the following day.

Try again I did. Every day I telephoned the Embassy, begging for special consideration because of my circumstances, but the answer never changed. Then I received yet another blow: it was pointed out to me that my movements were restricted to within forty kilometres of Moscow. If I was to see Mama again, then she would have to find me.

*

Meanwhile, I immersed myself in my work at the exhibition in the Park of Culture and Rest, Sokolniki, manning the stand by day and sampling Moscow life in every spare moment.

There were over 5,000 exhibitors from Britain attending the fair, representing every kind of industry imaginable. We were constantly besieged with visitors — reportedly about two million each day. These too were from every walk of life: businessmen, students and curious townspeople. I remember noticing the expression on their faces — a kind of bewildered frustration. Their dress also was different to what I was used to: neat and unassuming, but somewhat old-fashioned to a young woman with a passion for clothes, as I was. My own, numerous, changes of outfit were to provide many a humorous exchange with a group of students who frequented our stand over the next few weeks. One young man seemed convinced that the British government must have provided them specially for the exhibition.

I remember there being quite a lot of excitement at our stand just after the opening ceremony. A crowd had gathered to watch Mr Khrushchev pose for photographs when, suddenly, we heard a scramble of jostling and indignant voices. A group of Russian teenagers were fighting over my copy of the *Daily Telegraph*, which had been spotted in the wastepaper basket. I found later that the distribution of foreign newspapers was prohibited, which explains why my newspaper would sometimes mysteriously disappear from under the door of my hotel room.

Another of my duties as an interpreter was to arrange and attend business meetings between our company director and the Soviet officials concerned with import and export. At meetings such as

21

these, where we shared the same aims, I encountered the friendliness and courtesy of the Russians as I remembered them.

On one occasion, we were sitting round a large oval boardroom table in an opulently furnished import office. Just as I began to translate the first stages of introduction my voice suddenly disappeared. I panicked . . . but when I opened my mouth the words would not come. Mr Gold looked distraught – understandably, for he could not speak a word of Russian.

I quickly scribbled on my note-pad that it was pointless going on without my voice. Then a deep voice from behind said, 'Z' please, please let us continue later . . . let the young lady rest. She need some coffee . . . you work too hard!' A potential crisis averted, the meeting continued later to a successful conclusion.

*

Not all the Russians I came into contact with were so benevolent, however. It did not take me long to realise that I was rarely completely alone. No matter where I went a tall man, wearing a brown hat and carrying a navy blue raincoat over his arm, was never far behind me. It would take me almost half an hour to cross Sokolniki Park from our stand to the toilets, but my 'friend' would follow me there and back just the same.

Usually I could put him to the back of my mind but there were times when a glimpse of his lurking figure was the last thing I wanted to see.

I visited the famous GUM store one day. My duties as an interpreter were taking their toll on my vocal chords, so I bought some pastilles for my inflamed throat. I was alone, with time to spare, and decided to visit the magnificent domes of St Basil's Cathedral. The glorious architecture, priceless treasures, paintings and icons were almost hypnotic in their beauty. It would be impossible to describe my feelings as I worshipped in that ancient house of God. As I emerged, a little later, into the bright sunlight, I noticed that the KGB man had caught up with me again – another rude awakening from a moving experience.

He even turned up at the theatre. Our party had gone to watch the Bolshoi Ballet perform *Swan Lake*. The ballet was wonderful: I loved the haunting music and graceful forms of the figures onstage. I was so engrossed that I did not notice *his* presence until after the final act had ended.

Having spent the best part of my life in the West, I could not work out what exactly was happening. I tried to speak to him: who was he? And what did he want with me? I was not doing anything. It was like talking to an invisible man. I got no reply, not even a tacit acknowledgement in his eyes that he had heard me.

Only once did my silent shadow give me real cause for alarm. It was about three weeks into my stay and I was getting used to living in Moscow. In fact, I felt extraordinarily at home there, but always as a Westerner.

The food at the Ostankino hotel was not very palatable to most of the company executives and, as we were allowed to dine elsewhere in the city, we would go out to dinner most evenings. I enjoyed being able to use my own language in such situations, a welcome relief from the technical business of the day: where could we find good food in Moscow? Is there any Angus steak to be had in Moscow?

As a special treat for our director I had booked a table at the Soveskaya hotel where, we had heard, Westerners could find chopped shrimps and caviare. Although we were now in the beginning of June, the ladies were wearing fur stoles on their shoulders, their partners all in dark-coloured dinner suits, with carefully manicured hands. We had to share a table with three others, two men and a young woman. I noticed that one of the men had a strange accent when he spoke Russian, but thought no more about it. Mr Gold ordered a drink, then I saw him glance at the men, his eyes resting on the one with the strange accent.

'Does the name Guy Burgess mean anything to you?' he whispered, behind his glass. If it didn't then, it soon was to!

'It looks helluva like him. By Christ . . . it *is* like him.' His words were by now embarrassingly clear for anyone who cared to listen.

The man said nothing, but visibly reddened, his hand clenched on his chest as though willing himself not to answer back.

There was no stopping Mr Gold now. He had had a few whiskies and his nationalistic objections, not to mention more personal abuse, came pouring out. Guy Burgess responded to this aggressive outburst with restrained passivity. He stared at the table as if he wanted to disappear underneath it. Only when Mr Gold threatened to remove him forcibly from our table did the young woman in his company rise to her feet in indignation. She swept out, her companions following her in disgust.

I felt as though the whole world was staring. All around the room I sensed pairs of incredulous eyes and shocked whispers focus on us. And there, near the doorway, I spotted my KGB man. Fear gripped my stomach. What would he make of this scene? We had shared a table with a known spy – what would that make us in his suspicious eyes? Terrified that we would both land in Lubianka prison, we fled, leaving our meal untouched.

That night I lay awake, shivering in a cold sweat and regretting my foolishness in returning to this country. I knew from Mama's letters that my brother had served a lengthy sentence in Lubianka Prison because I had not returned home after the war. Many others I knew of had also found themselves there after being repatriated from Lienz by the British.

My own precarious position in the Soviet Union was never far from my mind. I knew that I should not come to any harm if I adhered to the Soviet regulations – only no one had ever told me what these were. My head by now was spinning with rules and regulations, rights and wrongs.

I had not disclosed to anyone that I had been present at the Repatriation, not wanting to risk the inevitable complications that would have arisen. What would happen if my secret were now to be discovered?

The next morning I was still in an emotional state and at breakfast announced to Mr Gold my intention to take the first available flight home.

His blue eyes darkened almost to the point of changing colour.

'The hell you won't,' he raged, his deep voice trailing off into a whisper.

To prevent me carrying out my threat he removed my passport from my handbag while I was out of the room, informing me that I would get it back when I had come to my senses. Needless to say, our conversation was strained for the rest of the day.

*

It was another busy day at the exhibition. As the visitors streamed past I searched, as always, for the loving face of my Mama. The precious days in Moscow were flying past without a word from home, my sole reason for going on.

Nearby, a group of small children with laughing eyes and Slavic cheekbones were playing with our colourful display of international flags. I watched them sadly, reminded of the kindergarten of my own childhood when I would ride a wooden horse bearing a hammer and sickle. There I too played with my companions, in the large hall, surrounded by posters of Lenin and other military heroes, or of the woman with a Lenin medal pinned to her chest, for bearing seven children.

It was nine thirty in the evening before the exhibition dwindled almost into silence; the only sound I could hear was the shuffling feet of the crowd streaming towards the exit. I was absorbed in my thoughts of Mama: her gentle voice, her bright blue eyes – perhaps they too would be clouded with troubles. Would she recognise me? I searched feebly for a picture of Papa's face as I had last seen it, but the image blurred in my brain.

As we crossed the dark expanse of Sokolniki Park, little flashes as people lit cigarettes glimmered like glow worms. A large, shapeless woman was twisting through the crowd, selling ice-creams and cookies.

In the taxi, Mr Gold was in one of his dogmatic moods. I studied his profile as he mused over the day's work. His intelligent eyes were fortressed by a heavy brow. He had a young man's face, contrasting oddly with his obese frame. He looked austere tonight, but as he relaxed his passion for telling amusing tales dissolved his stern exterior. He may have sensed that my normally irrepressible spirits were at a low ebb.

It is strange how the young can close the door on their troubles, if only for a while. The night that followed was one I shall never forget.

I was not feeling particularly hungry when we set off to the hotel Moscow for our evening meal. But as the night unfolded I absorbed the festive atmosphere around me. We shared a table by the dance floor with a Russian couple. The trolleys were packed with exotic fruit arranged on ornamental pedestals, iced cakes, Russian salads and porcelain dishes of red and black caviare. The place was crowded and as we waited . . . and waited . . . for our food to arrive we drank champagne. A friendly banter developed between ourselves and the Russian couple, ending with a glass of champagne being poured over my head because they did not care for the smell of my shampoo. By two thirty in the morning we all found ourselves in Red Square, in front of the Lenin Mausoleum, singing *Katusha* at the top of our voices.

Even at that time of night the capital's streets were bustling with pedestrians and taxis. I was to be on duty at eight o'clock, but instead of returning straight to the hotel we went first to admire the Metro, with its portraits and engravings illustrating Napoleon's retreat from Moscow.

No sooner had I fallen asleep, than I was awakened at six o'clock by a noisy telephone bell. Sleepily, I reached out to lift the receiver, yawning and trying to collect my senses. I tried to identify the unfamiliar Russian voice on the line. I could sense in every word he uttered how anxious he had been to trace me. At first I thought that someone must be playing a prank, then the voice repeated: 'Your Mama is with me at the Kievskaya. Could you come and see her now?'

'Now?' I said, gasping into the telephone.

'Yes ... yes ... and hurry,' confirmed the caller, in a tone that was both insistent and serious.

I asked him who he was, but did not recognise the name. When I pressed him further he merely stated that he was a 'friend of the family', but *I* could not place him from my memories or from Mama's letters.

It seemed strange that he had referred only to Mama; he never mentioned any other member of my family. Even more odd was the fact that my family knew nothing of my whereabouts in Moscow. There are millions of visitors to the capital each week, yet he knew where to find me.

For a moment I felt violently happy at my news, but when I tried to get out of bed I felt first faint, then cold, and my teeth began to chatter.

I was not allowed to leave the hotel on my own at any time, so I immediately phoned through to Mr Gold.

'Hello,' I said, 'I'm sorry to wake you at this unearthly hour of the morning but ... someone has just telephoned me to tell me that my Mama is now in Moscow and will be expecting me in an hour's time.'

There was a long silence before he replied in his loudest voice, 'Go to hell and sleep!' I burst into tears as the phone went dead.

Moments later my telephone rang again: Dougal Gold's tone sounded warm and sincere. He simply instructed me to order a taxi for six thirty, before breakfast. His mood was transformed ... but when I suggested that someone may be pulling my leg I was silenced by an indignant yell.

As I waited to leave my thoughts were far away. Another time ... another place ... .

CHAPTER TWO

THE STOLEN CHILDHOOD

Operation 'Barbarossa' — the German invasion of the Soviet Union — was launched on 22 June, 1941. Every man, and boy, who could walk was called up into the Red Army to defend the country. My Papa and brother Timothy were among them.

The first stone had been pulled away from the security of my little world. I was left with Mama and the other women and children on our sprawling farm in the countryside between Odessa and Pervomaisk, the scene of fierce fighting to come.

So much has passed between that time and the present that I remember little of my childhood before the war. It could not have been an easy existence: perhaps I was too young to understand the hardship and struggles of life under Stalin's rule in the thirties. Or perhaps, like all Russian children, I was cherished and protected by my family. Whatever the reason, my memories retain an aura of constant sunshine and loving indulgence.

*

Beyond the long pebbly path to our little gate acacia trees towered over the house. In the garden grew lilacs and beds of blue and pink delphiniums, almost ten feet high, and in between the narrow paths straggling clumps of hollyhocks and oleander proliferated. I loved to watch the birds and beautifully coloured butterflies attracted by the flowers.

I often used to climb our pear tree to measure which of the hollyhocks was the tallest, then wander to our small wooden postbox to collect the letters or, later, mysterious parcels from my big brother when he was an officer stationed on the Polish border.

We were very happy with small pleasures: bonfires in the cherry orchards, the sounds of the guitar, or harvest parties extending into the early hours of the morning.

I have an image of Mama in my mind, that same one from which I drew strength throughout the nightmare years in Germany. Had it been real — a photograph — it would by now be worn and curling at the edges. She is standing by the jasmine bush in a bright blue frock she had made by a local dressmaker. Her short, curly blonde hair is slightly obscuring her graceful eyes, glowing with kindness. To me, she had every quality a child could demand in warmth and security.

We would be woken each morning by the cock's obtrusive crowing. Before the day's work began in the whitewashed room, *babushka*, my grandmother, would cook our eggs on the iron stove, to be eaten with lavishly buttered bread she had toasted on a long metal fork. The samovar was always full of freshly made tea.

On Saturday mornings Mama would collect baskets of eggs and other farm produce to take to the market in town, while I took Mishka, my small horse, to escort dozens of ducks and ducklings to the river. It was my job, too, to bring them back in the evening.

I remember Papa rushing down to the main field to bring the cows in for milking. Krala was one of our most spirited and ferocious ones; she was also my special favourite. Many a time she kicked the milk pail, sending it flying through the air, only settling down when I would scratch her forehead.

Aunt Maria would gather the apples, pears and cherries for preserves. Some of the apples would also be pickled, together with cabbages, beetroot and other vegetables, to be stored in the underground cellar with the sacks of grain and salted meats for the long winter months. I can see my Aunt now, coming in from the garden to sit in her chair by the spinning wheel, next to the fireplace, and gently stroking my long hair.

Apart from the daily work on the land, Papa was also slowly rebuilding our outbuildings which were still scarred from the days of the Revolution. It was almost a sacred task in his eyes, and carried out with patience.

Sometimes, as a treat, we would go to the local picture-show, often having to scramble to get a seat for the black and white film.

Our home was a gleaming mountain of love, the kind of love I still feel most deeply inside me.

*

The war destroyed all that for ever.

Our home was not far from the frontier and lay in the advancing army's path to Odessa. It was not long before I witnessed the meaning of war, a concept which had previously been little more than an abstract word to my young mind.

As the German artillery drew closer, Stalin's army, ill-trained and equipped with little more than sticks and basic ammunition, were powerless to defend us. We ourselves could do little more than hide, trembling and praying for the noise of the battle to cease.

When we crept outside, hours later, a horrifying sight met my eyes: our sunflower field was flattened by the Russian dead. Even so, the German tanks relentlessly ploughed forward, their wheels clogged with corpses.

Often on my way home from school I had paused to gaze at this same field. The huge yellow flowers – swaying in unison – were like a beautiful poem, steeped in symbolism drawn from our folklore, of nature's cycle of life and rebirth.

And now ... I had never seen so many dead people. And so horrifyingly dead. I knew nothing of the carnage of war. Mama held my hand firmly; we were completely numb and wordless.

*

Life under occupation was, I suppose, tolerable ... to begin with. In some parts of the Ukraine the superficial changes introduced by the Wehrmacht were mistakenly looked upon as a form of 'liberation' from the harsh, unpopular Communist régime.

Before the Revolution, in my Grandpapa Polanski's day, we had been substantial landowners. The acres surrounding our farm had all belonged to our family. The Bolsheviks confiscated everything in the name of the people and formed a *kolckhoz*, a collective farm. They were not content with that: my Papa was imprisoned and his two brothers disappeared and were never heard of again.

I have no idea how long Papa spent in prison, or when he first went there. I do remember one day, as a very small child, Mama took me, accompanied by a friend in his *britchka*, into the town. I recall seeing a gaunt, bearded figure behind heavy iron bars. This, Mama explained gently, was my Papa. I was scarcely able to get to know him before he left to fight in the war.

We were allowed to keep one of the buildings on the farm for our family to share, together with half a dozen horses and six hectares of land. Our own plot was worked only after the allocated labour on the collective farm. We were permitted to sell any surplus at the market, but first a proportion of our produce was paid into the collective store, as a tax in kind.

I did not know any other way of life than this and loved our

31

humble home. We had plenty to eat and our close family unit helped us to come through any hardship which threatened us.

Now, though, with the men away, and constant fighting all around, the women were struggling to keep even part of the farm going. The fields were abandoned: we concentrated on keeping ourselves alive.

*

When the Germans first arrived they began by restoring people's property, even reopening the churches – ours had been turned into a cinema, though each Sunday crowds would still assemble to pray in the yard. School continued as before, with little interruption.

Mama and I were unluckier than most, a German captain and his men chose to requisition our home and its contents for themselves. We were flung out on to the road with no more than the clothes on our backs, until my cousin made room for us in her little cottage nearby.

Sometimes we would sneak back to the house when the soldiers were away during the day. Naturally, the intruders had found our cellar below the house and its painstakingly prepared store of food was quickly disappearing. We dared not touch any of that. But they knew nothing of the *second* one – outside the house – which Mama had concealed with earth and bales of straw before their arrival. It was this farsightedness which kept us alive that winter.

On one occasion we asked the elderly German captain's permission to enter the house. When I saw the bare walls my eyes filled with tears – our tapestries, icons and jewellery, even my brother's clothes which had been hidden in the attic, were all gone. I looked disbelievingly, first to Mama and then at the grotesque face of the captain who stood arrogantly, as if our house belonged to him.

From the earliest days of occupation we all worked against the enemy in any small way we could. I think Mama and the other women would take food to the partisans who were hiding in the woods. She never explained where she went. Young and old treated the Germans with silent contempt, avoiding them wherever possible and pleading ignorance in answer to their many questions, however mundane. We were not strong enough to fight them – but we would not make their job an easy one.

THE STOLEN CHILDHOOD

*

In the late summer of 1942 Hitler's armies swept down into the Caucasus and eastwards in the direction of Stalingrad.

In our part of the country a new type of soldier began to appear. Their evil-looking black uniforms and shiny helmets with the skull and crossbones sent deathly rumours flying round the houses. It would not take us long to learn that the Waffen SS were a force to be obeyed.

During the months that followed Hitler's organs vomited fire and destruction all over their occupied territory: the Gestapo ruled supreme and Germany fattened on the loot of the continent. Everyday life was transformed into a permanent state of anxiety. New rules were introoduced: many areas were prohibited and curfews imposed. It seemed to me that everything I would have liked to have done was forbidden.

Whenever the air was calm and free from the drone of aircraft I used to wander into the woods to gather mushrooms, acorns or the pretty little *venka* for my school botany class, unaware that these woods were out of bounds. I have an oddly salient memory of an SS commander – a huge, red-faced creature, wrestling with the steering wheel of his truck – yelling, '*Raus, raus. Ist verboten!*' before his truck floundered and crashed into an old oak tree.

Tales were rife of the Germans looting, raping women and children when and how they pleased, deaf to the cries of protest from mothers and grandmothers. But somehow we still looked upon Germany as a nation of culture: perhaps there were only a few madmen who could steal and murder.

We heard, too, of people disappearing from their homes and whole families being forced into trucks in full daylight. No one knew where they were taken. There were large Jewish communities in our area: we ourselves had many Jewish friends in Odessa and Pervomaisk. But it seemed that all our peoples were at risk – gypsies, Ukrainians and Russians.

As these stories began to be taken more seriously the women in our community busied themselves in keeping their children occupied, away from the SS men, and always in sight.

Our home was often full of young girls whom Mama would instruct in the arts of our traditional embroidery and tapestry. I would sit on my stool in the corner and listen to their girlish chatter, as children do. The names of our absent menfolk would be uttered, lovingly, and then Mama's voice would become tearful, for she could never speak of my Papa and brother without emotion.

I thought that she still hoped that our predicament would shortly pass, like the winds from the steppes which periodically ravaged the crops. But when I asked her when they would be coming home she could not answer me: her eyes, which were tenderly scanning my face, sank back to the tapestry she was holding on a frame.

*

We had our first encounter with the reality of such treachery in the autumn of that year.

I had developed an earache and, as school had closed temporarily, Mama decided to take me to the doctor, whose surgery was in the centre of Pervomaisk. It was a fair journey from our farm to Pervomaisk, but we thought little of walking even long distances, there being few motor vehicles in our part of the country. We would often get a lift for at least part of the way from a passing cart or truck.

It was almost dusk when the town came into sight. Not far in front of us we could see a crowd of people being marched under a heavy convoy of SS guards. A large number of German trucks had come to a halt in the middle of a barley field. They were packed with women and children. The last of the trucks was full of white-headed elderly men. The screaming women and children were unloaded and ordered to undress. With their arms stretched above their heads, they were made to parade, up and down, in front of the jeering guards. Some of the smaller children tried to cling to their mothers as they marched, naked, but an SS guard kicked them off before shooting them dead with his rifle.

Mama and I hid amongst the unharvested corn in the adjacent field, choking on our emotions. The SS guards then rounded up the second group of victims and when the blast of bullets hit their chests they fell, those poor wretches, like autumn leaves into the deep, long trenches.

We had to crawl on our bellies, panic-stricken, in order to pass the guards unseen. As we edged closer to the death scene we could not believe what we were seeing. Through the fresh virgin earth,

34

the victims' heads, arms and legs were still moving in the air, like worms burrowing in the ground.

The field was flanked by dead bodies; a plight of groaning voices assailed my ears from all directions. Mama held my head tightly while I vomited by the roadside.

We were obscured from view by a deep ditch. With heavy hearts we continued on our way.

*

When we reached the surgery there was no sign of any doctor. Instead we found a rabble of soldiers hysterically removing everything from the building and throwing it into their German truck. Mama recognised by their uniforms that they were Rumanians and Hungarians. Something was amiss. To avoid any trouble we quickly turned to walk in a different direction.

We were to stay with Maria Evanovna, a close friend of the family, but on the way Mama said that we should go into the church. I was too upset, but I had to go as Mama insisted that we should pray for the frightful sins that the Nazis had committed. All her life Mama had been led by an unshakable faith in God and had taught me from an early age to trust in his guidance and pray to him each day. At home religion was the centre of our life and I found it strange at first when I started school to be told that Christianity was evil, that Communism was the only true path towards a good and useful life. Mama had explained, as best she could, that I must not speak of these things outside the home. The prayers she taught me and the stories from the Bible were to be our secret.

There were few people entering the church: some elderly men with long hair and straggly beards quietly mumbling their prayers; young children in rags, ravaged by hunger, some with their mothers, others all alone. I felt a pathetic sadness hovering in the house of God. Mama made me bow as we lit the remembrance candles in front of the icon. Then, having prayed in silence, we crossed ourselves three times on the way out.

It was completely dark by the time we reached the large house where Maria Evanovna lived, alone as she was unmarried. A tall, cultured lady, she could not have been old at this time, but her grey hair gave her an air of mature sophistication. She was always smartly dressed, and wore a little make-up to emphasise the bright blue eyes in her distinctive oval face.

I always looked forward to visiting Maria. I used to enjoy her way of telling educational stories. The tragic story of the Romanovs was my favourite: she brought the Tsarina and her children so vividly to life, I could almost feel the pain of the Tsarevich Alexis' young life.

We found that most of Maria Evanovna's home, like our own, was occupied by German officers. They were attached to General Ohlendorf's unit. Nevertheless, she warmly welcomed us and ushered us into the dining room. She managed to produce two precious aspirins for my earache, and I soon fell asleep. I could only have slept for about an hour before I was woken by the blaring of German radio and guttural voices, and laughter.

'Bravo, that was a wonderful bortsch... and too many piroschki.'

The room was bursting with German soldiers – perhaps ten or eleven of them – relaxing after their daily activities. No one was listening to the radio and the floor was littered with empty bottles of schnapps, together with a tin of sardines and some half-eaten slices of very white bread.

My stomach was rumbling and I looked wistfully at the bread. One look at Mama told me that I must not touch it, so I rose and crossed the room to sit quietly on the cushion by the window, still feeling unwell and fatigued by the walk.

Mama and Maria Evanovna were too busy whispering their news to each other to notice me. Evanovna had recently returned from a trip to Simferopol, further south, where our Jewish friends were tracked and hunted like a terrified flock. She was very upset and crying because she was unable to find her close friend there – the neighbours had last seen her being forced into a German truck. Once the doors had been bolted, no one heard from her again.

Mama related our experiences on our way to visit the doctor. Evanovna's eyes widened: 'It simply means that when those Germans leave my home each morning... My God, they must be murdering people all day. Oh God! And then there is the night shift...'.

She pointed to the floor, under which two elderly people were hiding from the Nazis. 'Who are they?' I enquired. Mama swiftly slipped her hand over my mouth, glancing around the room. Her other hand firmly gripped my shoulder. 'Sch... sch...,' she whispered, 'you must not mention this to anyone – or we won't survive.'

*

We stayed with Maria Evanovna for a couple of days, until I felt well enough to make the journey home. By night we dozed in armchairs in Evanovna's room. For the women at least, real sleep was impossible with such a hostile presence in the house.

The evening after our arrival Evanovna invited the senior officer to share a Russian salad which she had prepared earlier in the day. A show of friendliness was essential to keep his suspicions at bay. We all sat in her room, around the circular table covered with a brightly embroidered peasant cloth. I remember it depicted a scene of fighting cockerels.

At first, the adults' conversation was the inevitable small talk, trivial and insincere – but safe. The bottle of vodka which the officer had brought with him was by now half finished. All of a sudden, he slumped down in his seat and began to gaze at the floor with a violent self-hatred. He started to speak of certain huge camps which existed for the extermination of people by the millions. I could not believe what he was saying; I don't know whether Mama or Evanovna did.

Ebbing deeper into his chair and grasping a large glass of vodka he inclined his head in the direction of the room filled with drunken SS men.

'Look at them. It is happening here right now. Ha . . . They had a hard day. If you listen hard enough, then you'll hear about the murders they commit each day as a matter of routine. And after the blood bath . . . they will organise wild parties in the victims' home. They gorge all the food that they can get their hands on . . . drink, smoke and then casually chat about their next group of shootings.'

He recalled also the contents of his family letters from Berlin, in which there was nothing but complaints for not sending back enough loot. Other Germans were sending so much more – paintings, precious stones, clothes and food.

The more vodka he drunk, the more bitterness he spat out. He spoke our language so well that he could have passed as a Russian. This SS officer, I thought, must be an educated man. How could he be such a barbarian? He did not mention the name of the village to which he and his men set light, watching the bodies turn into ashes.

Evanovna looked sickly white in the dim light by the table. We all faced each other in disbelief. How little we had understood the global fog of horror.

37

I made as if to leave the table, but the officer snapped at me to sit back down. It seemed as if he would never end his grisly accounts of the German 'triumphs' and how they had gained their victories all over Russia. It could not have been normal practice for an SS officer to reveal such matters to civilians, but he even described to us the motor vans which, he said, had been specially constructed to gas unwanted prisoners.

We thought that he must be too drunk or a bit touched in the head for all those revelations to be real. Yet, strangely, he seemed to be as frightened of his superiors as we were.

*

By morning we were ready to return to the farm. The warm atmosphere outside had spread a kind of silky softness over the buildings in the town. Evanovna was worried about our walk of many kilometres, so she had accompanied us for a short part of the way.

A mighty storm shook our cottage that night. Strong winds roamed among the trees, ripping fragments off the roof and scattering them in all directions. I shivered in my bed, covering my ears against the creaking timbers and the rumble of thunder, which tore through the sky to fade into a soft echo.

School was reopened the next day. In recent months we could never tell from one day to the next whether anyone would be there to teach us. Only one elderly teacher remained behind. He was German by origin, one of the early settlers or *Volksdeutsche* of whom there were many in our area. Such people were now avoided by the Russian population – they were quick to denounce those who helped the partisans, and provided information about our families to the SS men.

This old teacher, though, was harmless enough and kind to the pupils in his charge. Ironically, that day we had a German language class. I had chosen, before the war started, to study German rather than French.

I could hardly hear his words as he conducted the lesson at the front of the schoolroom. When he stood in front of my desk I could see him only in the black uniform of the SS. Piercing screams and shooting distorted my brain . . . My ambition to become a teacher had shrunk. From that day I refused to attend any further German class.

*

In November of 1942, icy winds cut through our bones and heavy snowfalls formed small mountains on a landscape which seemed lifeless and devoid of hope for the future.

I went for a walk along the River Bug. Mama would have been angry if she had known that I was out alone. She had forbidden me to stray beyond the immediate vicinity of the farm, anxious lest I end up in the brothel which, it was reputed, the Waffen SS had created in Pervomaisk. It was said that children of all ages were kept there and, for this reason, Mama kept me looking slightly dirty and unkempt. There were times when she hardly recognised me herself!

The snow crunched under my feet as I trudged closer to the river. On the other side, a mass of desperate men were dragging their limbs across the frozen fields. Then I noticed a large area, fenced off with barbed wire and closely guarded by German SS men.

As the men arrived at the compound they were thrown inside, where they huddled together, sheltering against the snow-filled sky. Eventually, they were so tightly packed that the backs of those on the perimeter were pierced and bleeding from the wire. The sound of heavy bombardment growled in the distance, beyond the railway embankment.

Those, once sane and happy, men had lost their balance in these terrible conditions. They must have starved – and walked – for many days. I could tell by their burning faces and their eyes, sunk deep inside the sockets. Their bodies were swollen with fluid and their clothes in shreds, and stained with sweat. Even so, many of the faces still retained a glimpse of dignity.

For some time I was transfixed, nearly frozen, and watched the cruel performance. In reality, I was looking out for my Papa's kindly face, or that of my handsome, tall brother, or my two fair-headed uncles on my mother's side and my two young cousins. All were somewhere in Russia fighting the war against the Germans.

After all my searching and heart-thumping I realised that it was useless – the spectres before me were beyond recognition. On my side of the river, other passers-by also stood, speechless.

I rushed home to tell Mama what I had seen. She called a few other women together and I led them back to investigate for themselves.

We wanted to do something, not just stand there, shamefully helpless. One woman, at the top of her voice, announced: 'We need to make vegetable soup – buckets and buckets of it.'

The women looked at each other, nodding in agreement.

'If we don't,' Mama added quietly, 'the men will not see the week out. God will help us.'

She crossed herself several times and, anxious not to waste a moment, began to walk home. The others followed her example.

Immediately on our return, all the women and children were divided into small groups and dispersed to dig out bags of potatoes and carrots which had been hidden underground for an emergency. We worked throughout the night until more than a hundred large buckets were filled with hot soup and numerous baskets piled with baked potatoes.

'Come and taste the soup. It smells good,' cried one flat-chested woman working with us.

'We'll soon get those men into fighting spirit again,' said the youth behind me, in his boyish voice. His long arms encircled me just as I was about to sit down on a bench.

'Could these men really be all right again? How many are there?'

I started to explain what I knew of the prisoners when, unexpectedly, the bench tilted and we both fell to the floor with a thud. A little laughter broke through the sombre night air.

It was almost light and for all we knew the sun might already be up, but hiding behind the dark clouds. Any tiredness we might have felt was forgotten as we strode through the valley of birch trees, crossing the bridges past the ruins.

We took a path which led directly to the field of prisoners and by the time we reached within ten metres of the compound our group on the road had swollen into a long column. Under the heavy snow, still falling, the leaves, like our *valenky*, were frozen stiff. But we kept going.

A German guard, clutching his rifle, yelled at us: *'Achtung! Achtung! Minen!'* (Attention! Attention! Mines!) His enormous belly expanded as his deafening shouts brought the rest of the guards running out from the nearby cottages.

Meanwhile, some of the women had already reached the west side of the fence, where they laid their buckets as near to the prisoners as they could.

The Germans reacted with a shower of bullets aimed at the buckets. Soup ran everywhere; women and children were screaming from fright.

Mama's thick quilted *valenok* had been pierced by a bullet. Hastily, she threw her basket inside the barbed wire before we fled. It seemed obvious that the Germans had their minds made up: the prisoners would either starve, or freeze, to death.

Once we had reached a safe distance I glanced back for the last time. The Germans had stormed on a small row of peasant cottages, setting them alight to keep warm. The flames leapt towards the sky, while the prisoners shivered, exposed to the now raging blizzard. Frenzied soldiers formed unearthly silhouettes as they drank vodka and danced round the fire, the snow melting under their feet. Others coarsely taunted the prisoners, indiscriminately staking their bayonets through the wire and firing their pistols into the air.

Mama and an elderly lady, her face twisted with hatred, stood beside me, as the blood-soaked snow deepened around the compound. It was a harsh reality.

*

The snow was five feet high by morning, totally blocking the roads to the main cities. Despite the weather, new drafts of Waffen SS men appeared from every direction. Thousands of them. Once again rumours circulated. Something was about to happen ... something big. But no one seemed to know what.

They wasted no time. A fierce hammer on the cottage door startled Mama and me. Before we had a chance to open it a rifle burst through, followed by the red face of an SS man, with small icicles tapering from under his nose. Roughly, he pushed Mama with his rifle butt and pointed to the rusty shovel my cousin kept beside the window.

Ten minutes later, we were trudging our way through the storm to clear snow at the crossroads, which stretch for many kilometres along the countryside. The German transport needed to reach their supply depot at Pervomaisk.

The snow battered against our faces and the wind whistled

around our clothes as we shovelled. We dug our way through to a large battalion of German tanks. They were motionless, the soldiers trembling, huddled between the crowded trucks.

Several hundred women and children were each made to clear one thousand metres of the snow on the road. And if our alloted workload was finished before darkness – there was plenty more to be done. By nine o'clock that night we could hardly stumble home for hunger and exhaustion: our hands ached with bleeding blisters. The final stretch of the long road having been cleared, the Panzer troops advanced in the direction of the River Don.

Russian watch fires fringed the horizon, pretty as a rainbow. The Red Army was not far away. The Germans piled their guns by the embankment in readiness for action, but no Russian attack took place and the Germans were left unchallenged.

December continued with unjust cold.

*

We were confused as to the progress of the war. We had no radio and our newspapers had long since disappeared. Hearsay was always unreliable and often contradictory. No news had reached us from Papa or my brother for countless months: for all we knew they could have been among the unfortunate prisoners we had found – or worse ... Some of them had shouted out their names and the areas they were from but amidst the confusion we recognised nothing. Mama relied on what she could learn from the partisans, or from others who had close contact with them, for occasional news about our armies.

As our life became more difficult, we spent more and more time in Pervomaisk, sometimes also going to Odessa – wherever the fighting was least fierce. Our food had almost gone: we could see no end to our unhappiness.

The towns, formerly filled with smiling pedestrians, rushing to the fruit markets or the factories, were now dingy and empty, ravaged by incessant bombing and shelling. Above the civic buildings garlands of swastikas flapped in the breeze. German tanks roamed the streets, their weapons swivelled towards the burning buildings; and from the flames the shadows of bodies rose into the air before falling again into the inferno.

When the wind blew the ashes of corpses towards us we cried, along with the cries from those mutilated bodies which lay trapped and buried beneath the rubble, beyond hope.

Odessa had become the centre of one of the main theatres of military operations. Soviet reprisals burst through the sea fog when least expected. German artillery rained shells on all the openings to the catacombs, which had become a base for the partisans. They poured oil and asphyxiating gases into the cliffs. They were never successful. Our people fought valiantly for survival, determined not to be overcome.

After each raid, the city looked as though a giant tornado had swept through it. It was usual to see old women, and children even younger than I, sifting through the debris, to bury the dead with dignity. Mama's friend, Natasha, died in this way. When her little boy had found her, he put his tiny hands around her face, slapping her gently. 'Mama, Mama,' he whimpered. 'Wake up, I'm frightened.'

As time went on we had no tears left.

*

Christmas Day arrived and the snowflakes fell fast to the ground. There were no church bells, no candles or news from our loved ones. The tiny Christmas tree we had placed in a privileged corner of the room looked bare and lonely without decoration. This year no gifts waited under the tree – the war had swallowed all of that.

We were lucky enough to have a few logs to burn and we sat in the glow of the fire listening to the roar of the planes that hovered through the night. This sound, and all it signified, terrified me and as I cried – as I did nearly every night – Mama stroked my hair holding my hand to comfort me.

We both were feeling the strain, and I was too young to give Mama the support she needed. I watched her wilt and her shiny hair fade to grey. But she never complained.

Two days later, on 27 December, it was my thirteenth birthday. We ignored the gentle tap on the door, assuming that it must be the German road patrol. It was repeated, but louder. Alarmed, Mama dashed to the door and flung it open. We knew better than to go outside: instead we waited for someone to come into vision.

A slight murmur came from the snow-covered path. We cautiously edged towards it and Mama struck a match, keeping me tucked behind her. Our eyes scanned the ground, eventually focusing on a pitiful heap a few metres from the doorway. A red mess seeped into the snow where Papa lay, semi-conscious but still breathing.

Throughout the night we took turns to massage his body. Our hands were aching, but we kept working and breathed on his face to keep him warm, talking to him about anything that we could think of. It was five o'clock in the morning when Papa smiled back weakly, uttering a little prayer of thanks.

Our hearts were filled with gratitude.

*

The Christmas break being over, I returned to school. My instincts told me that something was dreadfully wrong. As we tumbled into the classroom, the teacher, who was standing by the window, looked pale, his blue eyes stained with tears. He held a large bundle of pink postcards for girls.

The teacher let the noisy class chatter on for a few minutes. Then, in a strained, sharp voice he said, 'We have received a compulsory request from the German government which simply states: Those of you who were born in 1926, 1927, 1928 and 1929 must be ready to depart within twenty-four hours. There won't be much of a school left, I'm afraid, but orders are orders and we must obey them.'

I remember going temporarily deaf from fright. Some of the older children had left the school earlier in the autumn, but I did not really understand what was happening. My cousin was one of them. I had not forgotten the upheaval, the weeping mothers at the station.

An SS man had entered the schoolroom. One of my classmates was trying to explain that she could not leave her mother, who was bed-ridden, on her own. The answer to her problem was clear and precise: 'Those of you who fail to respond will be shot.'

For myself, I could not bear to think of such separation from my parents, nor could I expect them to come with me. I need not have worried: the Germans did not allow parents to accompany their children where we were going.

The school was closed and I returned home clutching my pink and white card and gave it, apprehensively, to Mama. She was inconsolable in her grief. My parents had a much better idea than I of the horrors that occurred in the Nazi concentration camps. It was decided that I would keep a low profile – perhaps I might be overlooked.

The first batch of children departed soon afterwards. No one came for the children on the farms as the days passed by.

The February snow storms danced on the frozen river; silvery crystals encrusted the conifers and the gilded domes on top of the churches sparkled in the sunlight. The arctic weather played eerie tricks with the light and the temperature continued to fall.

We kept warm with an infusion of herb twigs, constantly bubbling in the large samovar. It was the only thing that we had left in quantity. All that remained of our food was a small reserve of pickled vegetables.

Our army drew closer by the minute. We had heard that the commandant and his guards were talking of plans to retreat and prayed each day for a miracle.

The retreat soon started, but the gods of war would not leave us in peace just yet . . .

*

How well I remember that day. At our little cottage, the open window squeaked on its rusty metal hinges, letting harsh guttural accents and terrifying bursts of explosions seep inside.

Mama had already seen Waffen SS in their hundreds dragging screaming youngsters from their reluctant homes into waiting vehicles. She tried to speak, but her words turned into one mighty sob, her shoulders heaving under her black woollen dress. She knew then that we had only a matter of hours left of togetherness.

Oh, how distressing it was to feel her hysteria as it increased in intensity. I understood only that she loved me deeply, and all that she wished for was an assurance of my safety.

The clock ceased chiming.

Papa had managed to hobble into the tiny sitting-room, looking as though a great weight had been suddenly thrust upon him. He crossed straight over to Mama, his eyes brimming with tenderness, but unable to find any words to express it. He placed his crutches on a chair and they both took me into their arms, holding me tightly until Mama's tears gradually diminished. I felt the love and warmth in their arms as I had never felt it before.

Mama kept me by her as she packed my little bag for the journey. On the floor lay the clothes that I was to take with me and the items on the bed had been put aside for my return. I felt a sudden chill in my heart and a shivering sensation in the pit of my stomach. It looked as though we were preparing for my funeral, where instead Mama should have been making me a pretty dress, with satin ribbons and embroidered butterflies, for my first dance.

Throughout that night German and Russian planes dived in and out of billowing clouds of smoke and flames, while on the ground Waffen SS men ransacked empty buildings then set them on fire before they drove away for the last time.

Patiently, we waited for the return of the Red Army. Mama clasped her hands closely to her face. Her gaze lowered, she shouted, 'Where are you, brave soldiers? Protect us from these German pigs.' She was seized with impotent rage against the Nazis – who held the power to deny our youth as a giant would crush a plant in the palm of his hand. Her trembling hand fell on my shoulders . . . My world seemed so empty. I wished that I could die that very instant. I could see no future for us.

We hastened to the church as dawn was breaking, for the last time. I noticed that the pain in Mama's heart had destroyed even this source of solace. The church was packed with all who were left of us. My heightened senses swam amid the smell of incense and the sad refrain from the choir on the balcony. In the past, whenever our *batuishka* had faced his congregation his eyes were always ready to laugh, but now, as he genuflected and turned to address his people, they also were filled with tears.

I listened attentively, accepting every word he spoke as guidance from God. His sermons were always dramatic and left a deep impression on me. As he laid his small Bible on the communion table he took from inside it a crumpled piece of paper, found in the breast pocket of a dead soldier. Slowly he proceeded to read its scribbled message:

> I am sinking slowly from a terrible wound and my ears seem to burst with the noise of firing. The blood is pouring fast from my mouth . . . but I am swollen in triumph not to have been captured by the retreating Nazis. Those retreating Germans will rip out your guts without mercy. In Kiev, the Waffen SS had lined dozens of children up against the wall and then pushed a wooden bench against their bellies until their guts burst . . . They dragged their small bodies around the building. I believe they all died as they were doing it.

Suddenly, the tread of German jackboots echoed loudly on the hard snow outside; indistinct voices floated through the windows before the Waffen SS men stormed into God's house. They pounced on the priest, thrusting a revolver to his back, and seized the piece of paper from him. The people seated in the front of the church surged forward to aid the struggling priest, forming a confused heap by the altar.

Mama firmly grabbed me by the arm and pushed me outside the church. There too, in the yard, SS guards waited to disperse the crowds, clasping guns in their gloved hands, and stamping their jackboots – like mechanical soldiers. Their faces were grim and uncompromising. With intuitive clarity I saw shadows of a bleak future ahead of me, and there was no place to hide.

*

When we reached the cottage, Papa was shuffling back and forth by the window on his crutches, looking most perturbed; Aunt Mary was sobbing by the fireplace. We learned that the SS men had been along to collect me and would soon be back.

Mama folded me into her arms and squeezed me tightly against her. The tears in her eyes rolled down her chin and on to her dress.

I was standing in the hall shaking the snowflakes off my coat when three Waffen SS men forced the door open; I thought that my parents would go mad from terror. Mama pleaded with the smallest one of the three. I can still hear her frail voice: 'Please don't let her die ... please ... she does not want to die. Please don't take her away, she is only a child.'

I was by now screaming uncontrollably, when one of the SS men put one hand on my shoulder, jerked my chin up to face him and said, 'We Germans have only one penalty if you do not comply with our regulations – and that is death.' He pushed Mama, who was blocking the door, aside and she gasped for breath as her little body slid down the hall, stretched out in the shape of a cross.

Papa, too, was trying to protect me but a fat SS man with bulging eyes knocked him out of the way, ripping Papa's hand on the heavy iron door handle. The pain threw him off his crutches.

The door was now wide open and the snow outside drifted in to the cottage. Sickened and bewildered by the tyrants' behaviour, I put on my hooded grey coat and fastened the pompoms under my chin. As I stooped to pick up my small bag a screeching 'Halt!' and the even more ominous snap of a pistol shot into the floor threw me to the ground in shock. I quickly realised that the German truck was already waiting beyond the gate, and the precious moments with my parents were at an end.

Somehow, Papa managed to stagger to his feet, badly bleeding about the mouth. Without saying a word, he found his crutches and stood against the wall by the door. As the remaining SS man escorted me outside, his right hand still gripping his gun, Papa lifted one of his crutches into the air and lashed out at the SS man's back. The SS man retaliated with a volley of bullets; Papa screamed and then dropped heavily on to the snow, where he rolled pitifully, still screeching, 'Let her go.'

I turned my head for the last time to see Mama bending over Papa – the brave one who dared to insult an SS man. I thought that he was dying.

*

The truck sped away leaving milky clouds of snow behind us. An hour or so later, it came to a stop at its destination. I hardly recognised Pervomaisk station, as it was encircled by hundreds of both Waffen SS and Wehrmacht. The platform itself was packed with a host of children and adults of all ages, clinging to each other and holding hands. I recognised Marta and Nona, with whom I had become friendly during my visits to the town. Frantically, I waved to them but they disappeared into the crowd before I could reach them.

The cattle cars we were to travel in were crammed tightly with Jewish deportees towards the front of the train. The rest of us, including yet more Jews, were herded into the remaining cars. I stared at the nightmare all around me, but knew that I would have to do as I was told – any protest was futile.

The Waffen SS began to close in on me and I was swept inside one of the cattle cars and thrown against the side. When it could hold no more, the doors rolled shut and the bolt slid home on the outside.

CHAPTER THREE

STRUGGLE AGAINST DEATH

The interior of our cattle car was darkest brown in colour; a feeble ray of light only just filtered through a tiny slit, smaller even than a letter box. I thought I would suffocate, the air was so thick and poisonous.

I crouched in a corner on the straw and began to cry. How long I cried for my Mama before dropping off to sleep, I don't remember. My state of physical and mental exhaustion was so extreme that I must have slept for many hours. And as I slept I dreamed that I was living in a new, transformed world – like the Garden of Eden Mama had told me about. Yet through the peace a menacing laugh would assail my ears from time to time, distorting my beautiful vision.

When I woke up I was still in terrible distress and so cold that I could hardly speak. The people huddled around me were of all ages, from the very young to the old and frail. Most of the children were Jewish and had been taken from many different parts of Nazi-occupied territory. To begin with we were all helpful and courteous towards each other, exchanging names and trying to keep our spirits up, despite our fears. But, as time went by, our situation became intolerably morbid: tiny children screamed, and the sick moaned.

February north winds engulfed the train and a shroud of cold shivers descended on us. We were suffering badly from hunger as the limited provisions we had brought with us soon came to an end. We received no food from the guards, only one large bucket of water to share between us. Before I left the cottage, Mama had placed seven hard-boiled eggs in my bag. I was to eat one each day. By the time I had finished all seven, Mama had hoped, I should have arrived at my destination in some foreign country. My hard-boiled eggs, in time, were all eaten, and I no longer knew how many days, or weeks, were passing. The unknown journey seemed endless: the train kept moving further and further away from my home.

We had no toilet facility in our car. The older people were at first very agitated whenever they were forced to squat into the old bucket we kept, partly hidden by a grey blanket, in the far corner of the car. A metal mug was used to empty the urine through the tiny slit.

One woman, who was probably in her mid-forties and claimed to be a doctor, took charge of our car. The discipline and modicum of hygiene she instilled was to prove a vital factor in keeping most of us alive. But even she could not work miracles. I think that it must have been a week into our journey when the first death took place. A blonde fifteen-year-old girl from Uman died from acute dysentery.

The day after she died, the train came to a halt. The door was unbolted and some German soldiers came in to inspect the cattle car. By this time, we had lost all concept of normal human behaviour and as soon as the door was fully open we clambered over each other, rushing to fill our lungs with the fresh air. I longed to get off the train and be able to use my wobbly legs, but we had to stay where we were.

We must have been some distance from the main station, out of sight from the public, because innumerable long cattle trains stretched as far as I could see, each facing in the same direction as ours.

The guards came to each car and refilled our buckets with fresh water, but no food came our way. On the other side of the platform, meanwhile, a German hospital train also waited, full of soldiers who were eating, and drinking schnapps and who occasionally threw large chunks of white bread and *wurst* through the window and on to the rails. It was a cruel irony that we, who were starving by now, waiting for food when there was none to be had, could not even pick up their scraps.

It was not very long before the train jerked fiercely into motion and moved forward once more. Back in the darkness of the cattle car, one woman among us decided that she could take no more. 'Oh God, how much longer is this journey going to go on?' she cried, before swallowing a handful of sleeping tablets. The doctor tried hard to revive her, but she died later that night.

At this stage of the journey the guards were coming more frequently to inspect the car, at times twice a day. But they would do nothing to alleviate our hardship. Occasionally, an older traveller managed to bribe a guard with a piece of jewellery in exchange for a loaf of bread. Once the doctor gave her own wedding ring away to obtain a drink of cocoa for the sick.

Disease had taken grip of us all by then. I remember being told

52

that I had scarlet fever: I felt hot and was covered in red spots. What happened after that is no more than a blur in my memory and it may have been some days later that I became aware of someone by my side, wetting my burning lips. My head was resting beside the corpses.

I was aware of the silent life around me, and sensed that our journey was drawing to an end. Before daylight failed, I managed to peep through our tiny slit and gazed at the world outside. We passed through nameless glades – ones I will perhaps never see again, but will always remember. How I wished I could just stand on the grass, and hold a little blade between my fingers. Who knows what that little blade could tell me about the happier past it had known?

All at once, an immense flood of light blotted everything from my view and the train began to slow down. We must be coming to a town, I thought, reassured by the prospect that we were finally approaching civilisation. For some reason, I still half thought that I would be sent out to work, on a farm or in someone's home. My parents had spared me their deepest fears.

As my eyes became accustomed to the light they fell upon an eerie spectacle: a collection of weird huts surrounded by a forest of barbed wire and searchlights. I felt faint again and ploughed back to my little space, confused and trying to guess what the place could be. Whatever we had come to, it could not have been worse than that filthy cattle car.

*

When we climbed down on to the platform, a group of emaciated wrecks, hardly able to walk, arrived with more SS guards and took away our luggage. That was the last time that I saw my little bag. Many of the families who came with me had been led to believe that they were going to be sent to live on some sort of colony and had brought all their valuables with them. They, too, would never see them again.

An important-looking man then ordered curtly: 'All men on one side, women and children on the other.'

After the last of the cattle cars had been vacated and we were assembled, as instructed, on the platform we had to parade in front of the commandant, who stood with a handful of SS guards. They spoke to one or two of us as we filed past, before directing individuals, some to the left, and others to the right. This tactic was all new to us and we had no idea of its significance.

One SS officer – wearing the same uniform that I had learned to hate so fiercely in Russia – peered into my eyes and asked me my age. Before I could answer, he pointed me to the right road and I joined a sorry-looking crowd of people, wondering what was going to happen to us next.

We were marched in a long column, for a mile or so: the winter winds carried an obnoxious smell of burning to greet us. Auschwitz camp – our destination – housed some two hundred and fifty thousand innocent prisoners, fenced in by a mass of concrete posts and barbed wire, from which there was no escape.

We entered the camp and waited until our bodies were purple from cold for something to happen. Eventually, we were pushed into a large building resembling an aircraft hangar. The SS guards, who looked as though they were drunk, packed us together so closely that even the slightest movement was painful. More SS guards snapped out orders: 'Silence. Undress and leave your clothes over by the wall.' Obediently, we removed our clothes, wriggling against each other.

I looked around me, engulfed in horror. It was like one of those evil pornographic films – rows of naked girls subjected to the crude and dehumanising jibes of the despicable SS men. Our clothes and other personal items lay at our feet, a last reminder of home.

On the top of my little bundle, my small gold locket lay wide open, revealing its photographs of Mama and Papa. Their smiling faces stared at me gently as though they were trying to say something . . . I could not part with it and bent down to pick it up, but was noticed by a nearby guard. I felt the weight of his truncheon descend on the back of my head and collapsed on the concrete floor in a pool of blood. No one dared to help me. I had never been a robust child, even before the odious train journey, and could not withstand such merciless beating; thankfully, I fainted.

When I came to my senses, we all had to line up against the wall. Some, braver – or more foolish – than I, had tried to conceal their prayer books, photographs or other mementos from home. One young girl, whom I had heard someone call Klava, had torn a small patch of material from her dress and for this crime she was viciously beaten with an iron rod. The hawk-eyed SS man lifted Klava by the skin of her neck before dropping the poor girl to crumple to the floor, choking in her own blood.

We were next ordered into another place, much like the previous one, where our hair was cut off and placed in jute bags. We heard later that it was all sent back to Germany to be used in industry.

Even in the middle of such tragedy I managed to see the comic side of the picture we must have presented. Some of the heads had been shaven completely; others had big tufts of hair sticking up from the crown or beside the ears. We all looked so ridiculously hideous – yet some women even now retained their former radiance.

A compulsory medical examination was then carried out by the camp's SS doctors. It was a total farce: they did not appear to be remotely interested in our state of health. Much more important was the gold and diamonds that the older and wealthier prisoners among us may have hidden in their genitals. I heard of one such woman, an older Jewess, who was stretched out on a table with SS guards holding her down while the doctor minutely examined every crevice in her body. I passed through quickly, however, still dazed and finding the situation totally unreal. My only thoughts were for my parents: I was so grateful that they were not here to see me endure such humiliation.

Our 'reception' almost over, we passed in rotation under the freezing cold water which dripped slowly from suspended pipes in the shower room and had strong disinfectant applied all over our bodies. At least I was clean again. We were still dripping wet when we were flung outside into the freezing wind, and the snow whirled around our naked bodies as we queued for our camp clothes.

I cannot really describe which category my Auschwitz clothes belonged to. My odd-looking rough cotton dress, a pale sandy colour, came right down to my ankles. I was also given a tattered, dark-brown man's jacket and a pair of right-footed shoes, which were far too big for me. By that time I was feeling so cold that I was grateful even for these rags.

One particular moment, at this point, remains sharp in my memory. I remember looking at a small window and wondering if I could ever escape. But a strange voice from the shadows whispered in my ears: 'Stay put . . .'

*

I was to share a barrack with other women and children, nearly all of them Russian like myself. I had experienced discomfort during my last years in Russia and indignities throughout my journey to the camp, but *nothing* could have prepared me for such a place.

We were crammed inside like sardines. About ten of us were pushed into one bunk, only a couple of metres wide, and given one blanket between us. One of the guards struck my head, seemingly for no reason. I wanted to cry, but his insolent blow had angered me and I demanded indignantly to know why he had hit me, as I had done nothing wrong. Another blow quickly followed and I was told to shut up – I had a lot to learn.

It was pouring with rain outside and the water leaked through the roof, splashing on top of us. We were attacked, almost immediately, by thousands of fleas: I had never seen anything like it. I was still wearing my shoes but had no socks on my feet and it was not long before my legs were completely covered with them. In a futile effort to protect myself I tore a strip off my dress and covered my legs. The bugs and the filth on the floor contaminated the air so much that breathing was difficult. We did not sleep at all that night.

Two more girls, of about my own age, were brought to the foot of the bunk after being tortured: their angelic faces were black from the blows and through the patches in their threadbare garments purple bruises were in evidence. Such scenes of human misery were to become part of everyday life for me over the next year and a half, but I had still to realise how far man's cruelty can reach and could only stare in pity at the girls.

*

Much has been written about the atrocities committed by the Nazis in their concentration camps. Books about Auschwitz alone could fill a library. The facts are there for those who wish to read them – and they should, for the millions who died (not only the Jewish people) must never be forgotten. And yet . . . I do not wish merely to repeat what others have told. They, the older survivors, knew better than I what was happening around them. Though I grew up quickly, I was still only a child of thirteen and understood only what was relevant to me and the people nearest me.

For many years after the war I could not speak to anyone, not even my husband, about the experiences I endured; I am still choked with the scenes of inhumanity. For dates and numbers you must go elsewhere; the half-submerged memories I have pulled back from my subconscious tell only of one obstinate child's struggle to survive from day to day so that she might fulfil the promise she made to herself – to return home and be with her family.

*

One day ran quickly into the next. We rarely knew what date it was, as there was no way of finding out unless one was friendly with those in charge – and even then it was impossible to know whether they were telling the truth. But we knew when it was early in the morning because we had to get up for work; at night we were confined to the barracks.

Our breakfast would consist of a mug of brown liquid – it may have been some kind of soup or tea – and a tiny slice of black bread. Lunchtime brought another liquid, this time a murky grey colour, and in the evening we were given the same brown one as before, but no bread. Sometimes, when my hunger became unbearable, I would make myself think of Christ, nailed to the cross: I thought about the pain He must have suffered until I felt more able to withstand my own.

The washroom and latrines were the places where we exchanged news and views with other prisoners. It was the only chance that I really had to talk to people from other parts of the camp. It was here that I found out about new arrivals, who could be trusted and people and places to avoid. We explained to new prisoners how to keep out of trouble, just as others had done to us. Here, too, we would trade in the bread which we had saved, for a tooth brush or pieces of rugs, which had usually been stolen from 'Canada', the part of the camp where the SS sorted out their 'loot'.

The latrines, which were no more than concrete troughs, would accommodate up to three hundred people. The guards always made sure that no one stayed there longer than was necessary and would chase us out, brandishing large sticks. Waste water from the washroom was recycled into the latrines to flush away the excrement. More often than not, the pipe would become blocked and the prisoners were made to pump out the mess. The stench was terrible.

All this took place under the watchful eyes of the SS guards. I remember one occasion when I was in the washroom, sharing the pathetic trickle of water with Tonia and Irina, two girls from my barrack with whom I had become friendly. Irina was always obsessed with her dreams of a better world, and more outspoken than Tonia and myself in her criticism of the camp. She was speaking freely about her feelings towards the Nazis, telling us what she had heard about the treatment block, when she was overheard by the kapo. As a punishment we were put outside and forced to hold large stones above our heads. We stood there, willing ourselves not to stumble and so incur a beating, until our drooping eyelids were tightly closed with the pressure.

This was to prove a frequent method of punishment for even the slightest misdemeanour. We were convinced that the guards always picked on the Russian children in particular – I'm sure that was the case.

Unknown to us at the time, some of the British prisoners-of-war would watch us from the nearby punishment block. Not all captured soldiers were lucky enough to be protected by the rules of the Geneva Convention. One such was a Mr Bremner, who had been in charge of a commando unit which was taken by the Germans from behind the enemy line. He had been sent to Auschwitz and most brutally tortured during interrogations by the Waffen SS. While incarcerated in the punishment block, he and his fellow prisoners had nothing else to look at except the suffering faces of Russian children being punished.

Despite illness and the effects of his torture, he was sent out on construction work. It was not long before he was back in the punishment block, after it was discovered that he had sabotaged a new bridge by instructing his men to use the wrong kind of cement.

By an uncanny coincidence, I came face to face with this tall, fresh-complexioned gentleman one bright sunny day a few years ago. He strode up to me, as I was doing my shopping and peered curiously into my face.

'Well, well,' said Mr Bremner, holding his fishing rod over his shoulder. 'I did not think it was possible to see *you* here in Broughty Ferry – a long way from Auschwitz, thank God.' I was taken aback, not knowing that he had been watching me for some time, and told him that I did not recollect seeing him in Auschwitz.

'Oh, of course you won't remember me from Auschwitz days . . . how could you? It was a long time ago.' His face became taut. 'I used to watch you kids when you were holding stones above your heads, and sometimes during the roll call. I would recognise your eyes anywhere, a hundred years later! There is something about your eyes... a certain sadness...'. How he could recognise in me that scrawny child I must have been, I cannot tell; it may have been the distinctive birthmark I carry on my forehead. In any case, it was an emotional meeting and we spent many hours recalling various incidents in our shared past.

*

The roll calls were almost as much an ordeal as our punishments. They could occur at any time of day or night and we would stand, sometimes for hours, waiting for someone to arrive to count the heads, or 'select' those of us who were no longer fit for work. We all knew that selection meant certain death and would be thankful for the days when we had already been put to work before the main roll call.

In winter we would shiver dreadfully, exposed to the rain and snow, but in the summer the hot rays from the sun would only add thirst to our hardship. Meanwhile, we had to watch the SS guards standing over us, drinking from bottles or pocket flasks. It was at times like those that I would bless the rain, when raindrops would roll off my cheeks and into my mouth.

Just before I came to this earthly hell, when I had been tense and frightened, Mama and I had had a long talk. She had given me this advice: 'Walk tall, child. Hold your head high – use your charm instead of venom. God will guide you with the rest.'

Where, I wondered, was God right now? With all the violence, the grievances and uncertainty we had almost forgotten how to talk properly and our heads would dangle on our chests, for fear of being clobbered by our captors. And yet... I still went down on my knees each night as I did at home and prayed for the day that I may be with my loved ones again.

*

It was well known in the camp that all new arrivals were allocated to one of two main destinies: one was liquidation and the other was to be worked to death. Either way there was little or no chance of survival. I and the other inmates in my barrack had been the

59

'lucky' ones as we stepped off the train: at least our *hope* had not been taken away from us.

When we were sent to a different place of work, we never knew if we would return alive at the end of the day. The SS guards never failed to remind us that we were very privileged children to have been left alive and chosen for work – and not to have been swallowed by the suction of the gas ovens.

Most of the girls I knew worked in 'Canada' or at scrubbing out the latrines or the filthy barracks. I spent my first few months doing the latter. Tonia, however, worked in 'Canada' and, on a night, would describe the jewellery, diamonds and furs she packed into uncountable boxes before labelling them to be sent to Germany. I was only there once or twice – I even saw old sewing machines, which must have been carried, full of hopes for the future, from some unknown home. As more victims arrived at the camp, more trainloads of treasures were despatched to Germany. It would be interesting to know where my own little bag went to.

One day, I was sent to help out in the infant section. The scenes I saw there were pitifully sad: endless rows of empty prams, infants' shoes – enough to supply a whole city – and pile upon pile of babies' dresses, some even stained with blood. There were moments when I imagined that the prams were filled with babies and almost heard their cries for mercy.

Many women, from all types of background, became hardened thieves, even though they knew that anyone caught stealing would be subject to horrible punishment, or death.

Nadia and Nona, who shared my bunk, were sent to work in the notorious Buna factory, which manufactured rubber, among other things. I was to learn from them just how much toil a human being could stand. I watched them fade away, working until their last breath. One night they did not return: it was said that their lives had been terminated by a simple injection of phenol.

*

However dreadful my experience of Auschwitz was, I fared better than those who were sent to the Birkenau compound – another part of the camp. Sometime in June 1943, a large transport from Czechoslovakia arrived. We thought that we might have been sent to help the new prisoners hand over luggage, but instead they were allowed to take it with them to Birkenau.

We children were always eager to speak to the new ones. We never knew when we might find someone from our own districts who might be able to tell us something of our families. I got to know one of the Czech boys from that transport. He was the same age as me and spoke Russian, and over a period of several months we chatted to each other whenever we could, he on one side of the barbed wire and I on the other. I envied Mishek: he still had his thick, dark head of hair and lived together with his family, who even kept all their possessions with them. I thought that they must have been a special category of prisoner to be so privileged and I used to tease Mishek about being the best-dressed prisoner in the camp.

Then, one day, he came over to his usual place behind the barbed wire and threw a little bundle across to my side: it contained his shirt and a pair of shoes. In a quiet voice he said, 'I won't need them any more. My parents are already in the gas chambers and tomorrow, when you see the flames from the chimneys, it will be my turn . . . and I will be thinking of you.'

I turned away in sorrow and held the tiny bundle close to my heart with a prayer – I had no tears left.

I never saw Mishek again. Each time I went near our meeting place I trembled with cold shivers: I could not believe that he was dead. We had dreamed of going together to visit the places he described to me: the ikons, paintings and sculpture in Prague's teeming galleries; or to enjoy the symphony orchestras my ballet teacher had spoken of, in some Moscow auditorium. We were at the age when we longed to learn – but our youthful exuberance was crushed with a thundering violence, through no fault of our own.

I find it sad that no tombstones exist in Auschwitz: the dead remain anonymous and uncounted. At the time many believed that the barracks were full of ghosts, the spirits of those who were brutally murdered. It was said that the spirits had been known to intervene on behalf of some unfortunate prisoner.

I remember one much talked-about incident in my own barrack. Although our SS masters threatened and punished us more frequently than we would have wished, we were less afraid of them than we were of some of the older inmates and kapos, or *blocovas*, as we called them. The *blocova* in charge of our barrack had, on this occasion, ground the face of one of the prisoners into a bowl of boiling liquid. A fierce struggle ensued and the *blocova* started to cudgel the woman's head with her bludgeon, trampling on her body. Suddenly, the bludgeon slipped from her hand, as though someone had said: 'Enough! Stop, stop this appallingly brutal punishment.' The *blocova's* face turned white like snow and she began to screech threats and obscenities at the top of her voice, but remained, nevertheless, skulking by the door, like a hunted animal.

*

One morning, we had not yet left the barrack to go to work when a roll call was ordered. In the men's enclosure one barrack existed for boys of fifteen and sixteen years of age, most of them Russian. During the course of the roll call about two hundred of these boys were ordered to step out of the rows and made to undress. For many hours they waited, naked, with their clothes at their feet, until the trucks came to pick them up. When afternoon came there were only a few left. Silently, we watched the trucks pass by, heading in the direction of Birkenau. The most dreadful cries were carried through the air as each shouted out his name, in the hope that someone might pass it on to his relatives. Vovka Breznew was one of the lucky ones: I met him later in the washroom where he told me how he and ten others had been hidden by the Polish men and thus escaped selection.

That evening, our barrack was full of weeping mothers whose thoughts were with their children. No one slept that night; we watched the flames belching from the chimneys. Like the waves in the sea, life expectancy in Auschwitz was unpredictable.

Some time later, another two hundred of us were pushed into trucks, waiting outside the barrack, even before we had been given our liquid breakfast. We too, were all children, between the ages of thirteen and fifteen. My heart thumped so fast that I could not count the beats. The most fearful thoughts hovered over my mind – that we also might be heading in the same direction as the boys. Instead, the trucks speeded away from the camp altogether. There was a lot of traffic on the road and the headlights from the trucks illuminated a signpost which I read as pointing to Crakow.

It was winter, and still dark when the trucks braked to a halt beside a long row of houses. They were stone-built and apparently deserted, with avenues of trees lining either side of the street. A deadly silence reigned. I felt the ghosts touch my cheek as they quivered in the dark. I thought, too, that this must be the place where we were going to be shot.

An SS guard yelled at us, *'Raus, Raus, mench!'* as he held open the gate which led directly into one of the houses. Thirty of us marched into the hall and stood on the pine-clad floor. It was covered with puddles of blood – still fresh and not yet congealed. The walls along the staircase were also splashed with blood. We were given buckets and instructed to fill them with water and clean up the mess.

Throughout the house portraits and family photographs framed in silver were displayed on top of beautiful period furniture: the unfortunate family must have been considerably wealthy. Even while we worked, SS men ransacked the house, taking what they wanted and throwing the rest into large sacks. I found out later that this house was one of thousands that prisoners were sent to clean after SS men had murdered entire families during the night.

We worked our way through the house and I reached the bathroom. I was just about to empty an oval-shaped linen basket when I was horrified to find, among the bloody linen, a tiny murdered child, its brown curly hair forming a halo around its head – like a cherub. I screamed and screamed. Even the hardened SS guard could not stop me from screaming, until my throat was choked and my lungs were aching. So there it was, another little Bach or Mozart had been killed by the monstrous SS men. As I stood over the child I felt as though I was surrounded by angels, overshadowed by some mystic figure holding out symbolic garlands towards me. Whispering voices seemed to prophesy: 'You will survive . . .'.

The shock had disturbed my mind so much that even when our long-awaited food arrived it could not calm the turmoil of my thoughts. It was late into the darkness by the time we had finished scrubbing the house. Listlessly, we climbed into the truck for the rough ride back to the camp. We were so cold, tired and hungry that we all fell into the bunk fighting for spaces, back in the thick nauseous air of the barrack.

Mama came into my thoughts. Oh yes, the word 'Mama' is the most beautiful word: all over the world it rings out its meaning in every language. It is the infant's very first word. 'Mama' – who has the kindest hands and a faithfully loving heart. Her love *never* dies.

*

Everyone in Auschwitz was mortally afraid of hospital 'injections'. The sick would drag themselves off to work, almost as anxious to avoid the hospital as they were the gas chambers. You could not be sure you were safe even if you escaped selection at the roll call. Dr Wirths, for example, had a habit of choosing his victims from the barracks.

One day Dr Wirths and his helpers strode into our barrack and looked around at the people remaining there. I was on my knees at the time, trying to clean up some of the dirt. He pointed his fingers at me and another girl, Elena. Frightened, I pretended not to have noticed him, but one of his hospital helpers pulled me off the floor by the ear and Dr Wirth's hand clamped down heavily on to the back of my neck. 'You will do for a specimen,' he said, with a certain degree of command.

I did not know the meaning of 'specimen' at the time but was quickly informed by one of his helpers, a middle-aged Hungarian woman – rather too well-fed by Auschwitz standards – that we had been selected for 'hospital treatment' tomorrow. I did stop to wonder why *I* should have been chosen: I had never complained of any illness and, anyway, knew of no facilities at the hospital to care for the sick. At this point, I really thought that my young life had come to an end.

About two hundred and fifty of us had to report to the hospital block the following day. With each step I took I felt my blood going cold and my knees start to tremble under me. Our escort snapped out, 'Fall in', and then she prodded my back with her bludgeon. Although the pain was unbearable, I somehow found the strength to run ahead, out of her reach, accepting my fate, without tears, as God's will.

I was being sent to live amongst the living dead: countless jaundiced faces wedged against each other, dressed in rags. In the isolation block skeletal beings piled up against the windows, shaking their fleshless hands at the new passers-by. What message were they trying to tell us? Perhaps the true meaning of Nazism.

One of the hospital barracks we passed was so overcrowded that some patients had to lay outside, partially covered with blankets and burning with fever. Their groans were reduced to mere whispers. The door was left open and revealed a corridor which was also packed with the sick. A queue of ailing women waited for consultation all day long, their tense faces painfully distorted: they knew that hazardous diseases such as diphtheria and scarlet fever would condemn the patient to the gas chambers.

As we passed through the queer world of barrack-alleys we met a wave of swastikas and gestapo caps – the black shadows of the Waffen SS men. They seemed curiously incongruous in this chaotic wilderness, like a special school excursion.

My already fluttering heart did not know how to beat any faster when we arrived at the experiment block and saw what lay in store; large beads of sweat streaked down my tiny body like a heavy rain. Female children lined the whole wall. They lay, naked, their legs strapped to vertical iron rods which were fixed on either side of each bed. This was the block and its demonic machinery for experimenting on humans – the Nazis must have had more respect for their animals than they showed to us.

I felt a sudden surge of blood to my brain and fell heavily to the floor. I do not remember how long I lay there, unconscious, but when I opened my eyes I was surrounded by even more trolleys of young girls, jammed tightly together in the centre of the building. I myself was tied to an operating trolley, with lacerating pains shooting through my body. I wanted to cry out, but my throat was choked and my screams were stifled before they even left my mouth. A man in a white coat was inserting a large needle into a vein in my right arm and a bright red liquid flowed in folds and waves through the long tube which was attached to a bottle suspended from the iron rod above my head.

It was much later that I learned that this experiment was designed to induce and then arrest the menstrual flow in order to monitor its effect on the ovaries. A young Jewish girl, Eve, who came from Poland, told me a few days later that the experiments we were subjected to were carried out on behalf of a German pharmaceutical company, IG Farben. She had been interred on the block for several weeks, but I only knew her for a week or so before she disappeared. I never saw her again.

I have had problems all my life as a result of these experiences. Research has shown that in nearly all the female survivors the ovaries retained an abnormal shrinkage. Many children of my age never reached the normal process of menstruation.

At the time I had no idea what was in the bloody liquid which was so hurriedly pumped into me. I submerged myself into a deeply felt prayer and tried to block out my panic. Suddenly, I felt my leg being raised by a white-shoed SS nurse. She was about to insert yet another strange-looking instrument. I was having none of it and a strength I never thought I had reappeared from nowhere: I kicked over the tray of instruments, and for a time no one could get near me. The SS orderlies summoned by the nurse eventually held me down so hard by the ankles that, to this day, a deep purple mark (in the shape of three large thumbs) can still be seen.

Dr Wirths (not that I knew his name at the time) stood near by, smirking during my struggle. Once I had calmed down, he inserted a needle in my ankle, and a thin wire which was connected to a box which looked something like a radio. He never spoke a word and I was surprised how he tolerated my obstinate resistance to their enforced 'treatment'.

Those white-coated physicians seemed fascinated by the horrific transformation of the young females in their charge. I caught a glimpse of Raya, a girl from my barrack, who was by now almost unrecognisable. Beside her lay many other young children: their faces shrivelled up like old prunes, their hair like straw. Their bushy eyebrows indicated a long stay and some of them had huge pregnant bellies.

An unbearable homesickness overcame me. If Mama only knew what miserable torment I had endured ever since I was taken away from my homeland. I lay and wondered bitterly if Mama's comforting arms would ever hold me again. I wished I could only get in touch with my family, even though I knew they were powerless to help me – until our day of liberation came. One day more of these poisons might make me permanently sick or even end my life – and no one would ever know.

Between experiments, when we were left alone, those of us who were able would talk to each other, sometimes shouting feebly to the beds across the room. We had learned, by now, to communicate with anyone, whatever their nationality. Our conversations had not changed much: our names, where we came from and whether we had any parents or brothers and sisters in Auschwitz. Only now we described, too, how our heads hurt, or our stomachs and speculated on what our individual experiments might be meant for.

Many more, of course, were beyond their days of meaningful communication. One twelve-year-old girl whom I had noticed was heavily pregnant on my arrival, wandered aimlessly round the building – a barely living corpse – until one day she was not to be seen.

A few of the stronger girls remained on the block long after their ordeals were over. They would make themselves useful folding and unfolding bandages, rarely revealing their true identity. There were four girls in particular I often spoke to, who used a different name every day.

I had lost none of my inquisitiveness and kept a close eye on what was happening around me, asking endless questions whenever I saw anything I did not understand. We had no idea who the doctors were, as they were never addressed by name. But once the war had ended, I recognised many faces as I followed the news reels and the papers during the trials and controversies which ensued.

One morning I saw, from the corner of my eye, Dr Capesius, an SS pharmacist and a senior director of Bayer IG, conferring with Dr Klein. Dr Capesius was holding a large glass container which was filled with liquid. Inside floated a human heart looking as if it wanted out from its isolation. The place was full of such containers, holding strange meaty objects. Dr Klein then examined another and held it up to the light, tilting it up and down before stating simply: '*Das ist genug*' – that particular experiment had come to an end. He walked past my friend Roda's bed and chalked a large cross on the board which was attached at the bottom. I asked the girl next to me what it meant. Her answer was simple but shattering: 'The life of the person will be void.'

The block seemed silent for a moment and then I heard heavy footsteps coming towards me. A white-coated SS doctor took a syringe out from his pocket and plunged the needle into my left arm, waiting until the scarlet liquid had filled the glass tube three times before jerking it out and placing it on the moving surgical trolley.

An SS nurse then arrived with a bowl of soup and laid it on my chest, the only space she could find amid the tubes, wires and other contraptions. I could not summon much enthusiasm for my unexpected food, not knowing whether it contained nourishment or sedatives. I trusted my fate and emptied the bowl. Sure enough, some moments after the liquid had entered my gullet, I became drowsy and the human relics in the beds opposite began to sway from side to side.

It was nightfall when I came to: whether or not it was the same day I cannot tell. I became very afraid, newly conscious of the combined smell of rotting flesh, disinfectant and soiled mattresses.

My swollen arm throbbed mercilessly and my vision was blurred, yet I dare not ask for help.

All through the night I lay awake, listening to the children's delirious moans and lamentations. I detected a difference in their voices – they were the new replacements for the next programme of experiments. I still remained in the centre of the room and beside me stood a trolley holding an abundance of surgical instruments, syringes and brightly coloured tablets being prepared for more tests by an SS nurse.

Dr Capesius and his assistants made a dignified entrance the next morning, while the SS nurse shouted '*Achtung*!' and then stood to attention throughout his inspection of the new victims. The death administrators gazed dispassionately at those beautiful young girls ... Oh yes, they were staring at the rosebuds before their damaged petals shrivel up and die. In their immaculate SS uniforms they strode along the rows of beds, picked up some of the charts and jotted down unexplained mysteries.

My pus-ridden ankle was angrily swollen, and poison had set in, but the SS team did not bother about that. They gouged with a scalpel on my left leg and extracted a fresh chunk of flesh for one of their experiments – the wound has never completely disappeared.

I was suffocating in the gloom of my surroundings; for the first time I wanted to die as quickly as possible. The piercing pain and my soaring temperature made me barely notice what else they did to me after that. But nature is wonderful ... and chose to heal my weakened body; within a few days the raging fever had subsided and the pain lessened. My remarkable recovery had surprised even my new young neighbours, who had also thought that the rubber-wheeled trolley on which I lay was ready to be declared 'void'.

I tried very hard to summon some happier thoughts – a splash of colour into the grey of my existence – and formed a picture of Mama and Papa's smiling faces. Then I recalled my old playground, packed with my school friends – we were all so happy.

The sound of heavy boots once more interrupted my thoughts and I felt a sharp probe sting my chest: it was the distinguished-looking Dr Capesius. His facial expression made me wonder for a moment whether he might show me a little kindness – but I was mistaken. Like a robot and without any word, he held my teeth apart and placed a handful of tablets in my mouth. When

I could not swallow he pressed on my throat with his clumsy fat hands and when I vomited he simply started again with a different type of tablet. I was staring at him wide-eyed; I wanted to ask for mercy but the words did not want to come out. Unpitying, he chose not to hear my whimpers and seemed to smile with self-satisfaction.

After he had finished with me my eyes continued to follow his progression round the room – armed with rubber tubes, glass containers and swabs – as he examined the new arrivals. Flurried screams would echo across the block as each experiment ended: for the long hours to follow not even God in heaven could save those children from his cruel hands – not until their experiments were completed.

One of the voices I would have recognised anywhere. It was little Hester, whom I had last seen at the station. Her long brown hair cascaded from the trolley which Dr Capesius had halted in the centre of the room. (When Hester had reached the ramp I remember that he had patted her on the head and separated her from her parents.) I do not know what sort of tests Dr Capesius was making on her, but I knew that whatever it was it must have been very painful as she was twisting violently on the trolley. Later, I saw him fill a syringe with liquid and plunge the syringe into a vein of the screaming Hester. It took only seconds before her screams were silenced for ever.

In May 1965, at the Frankfurt trials, one of the prosecutors, Henry Ormond said this of Dr Capesius: 'As to the doctors who so willingly destroyed life in Auschwitz . . . never in the history of mankind has there been such corruption, perversion, and bestialization of the healing professsion as in Auschwitz among the heads and assistants in the medical service of the Waffen SS. The defendant Capesius was one of the biggest ghouls.'

The Frankfurt court found it particularly despicable that Dr Capesius had enriched himself with the property of the murdered victims.

After 1950 he had his own pharmacy in Göppingen, a cosmetic salon at Reutlingen and by 1958 his yearly profits were 400,000 Deutschmarks. Asked where he got the money for the business, Dr Capesius said, 'I have no cause to feel guilty'.

Lawyer Ormond said that 'Auschwitz offered great opportunities for robbing the dead, and for this reason alone the defendants stayed there and engaged in mass murder. They preferred unlimited mastery over the defenceless, and they were intoxicated with power and blood. One shudders to think that those who now sit on the defendant's bench, were for twelve years looked on as the élite of the German people and thought of themselves as such. One is ashamed on behalf of the Germans for having accepted this. The majority of the German people do not want to conduct any more trials against the Nazi criminals. But as long as certain German tabloids call for the death penalty for taxi murderers, but demand that proceedings against the Nazi mass murderers be dropped, these trials have to be continued. All those who, like these defendants, had a part in the unbelievable brutal mass murder of millions of defenceless people will have to face German courts. If the survivors of the hell of Auschwitz could no longer bear witness – and certain circles are waiting for just that – then Auschwitz would become nothing but a legend in a short time.'

I often think that if those SS murderers experimenting on my body as well as my mind had suspected for one moment that I would survive and even attempt to write about their atrocities, then they would have used that same phenol injection on me as they did on Hester.

*

The sun was shining and the smell of cabbage soup in my nostrils encouraged me to sit up. Everything around me was dirty, hostile and ugly; nothing attractive diverted my eyes.

My attention fell on a pair of twins who were being escorted to the other side of the building by a Waffen SS man. They had the most beautiful long blonde hair and chatted cheerfully in some Slavonic language as they passed. The SS nurse took charge of them and led them towards the first two empty beds she could find.

Shortly after midday, Dr Mengele, another of the doctors on the block, arrived, went straight over to the twins and began to administer a blood transfusion. With his SS assistants, he watched the twins' skin change to purple. One of the beautiful twins vanished sometime during that night, while the other was forcibly fed with a watery soup by the SS nurse, until her tiny stomach looked as though she was six months pregnant. I never managed to learn their names.

I understood, even at my age and ignorant of medicine as I was, that these experiments had little or no scientific value. Dr Mengele was like a boy with a beautiful butterfly, who lacerates its lovely wings and then tramples its tiny body to bits.

It was ironic that the doctors worked purely to further their own ends when there were so many debilitating diseases raging round the camp. At one point a complaint was made to the camp's commandant concerning the prevalence of a terrible gangrenous disease called 'noma', from which many of the children were suffering. The commandant suggested no remedy: 'You are complaining of difficulties,' he replied. 'Just look what IG Farben have achieved in a year.'

It is hardly surprising that IG Farben made rapid progress in their research, when they had thousands of unpaid prisoners at their disposal, working day and night until their last breath had gone. When else in history, too, have there been so many, like myself, subjected to wicked medical experiments and then cruelly disposed of – only to further the Nazis' knowledge of human endurance, resistance to hunger, cold, heat and high altitude, the reproductive system and tropical diseases?

The terror and desperation of those days still flashes before my eyes and the obnoxious odour of burnt flesh in the stale atmosphere lingers in the air.

*

It was yet another test they were carrying out – a hormone test for Bayer's urgent research. My mind was preoccupied with thoughts of death and I wondered how long it would be before my turn came.

I felt a gentle hand come to rest on my forehead.

'Oh God, no,' I exclaimed, thinking the worst was about to happen. Instead, I heard with joy the soft tones of my mother tongue: '*Ot kuda te?*' (Where are you from?) It was a Dr Dmitrovna, or some similar name, whom I had never seen before. She spoke quietly to me and insisted that any kindness which she may contribute must remain confidential, especially in front of the SS staff. I soon discovered, when she conversed with the SS nurse, that her capabilities in speaking German were still very limited, and she had to rely on the patients to interpret for her.

We were interrupted when Dr Wirths returned for his inspection. A Polish girl, Jana, had fallen at his feet, begging him to let her out from this hell. Dr Wirths kicked her on the head so hard that he cracked her skull: his boots were saturated with the spurting blood.

Dr Dmitrovna's expression turned into a powerfully stern one and I knew that she meant me to understand that I must not say a word. Dr Wirths proceeded, surprisingly, to clean up the mess himself, while Jana was transferred to the medical block.

Once the SS doctor was out of the way, Dr Dmitrovna enquired about my family. I told her about my brother: that he was an officer in the Soviet Army fighting somewhere to free us. For some reason she began to speak of ten thousand Russian prisoners-of-war who were transferred from Lamsdorf to Auschwitz. By 1942, she told me, most of them had died from exposure, undernourishment and various other ailments; no doctors had been allowed to treat anyone among them – they were left to starve to death. Afterwards she had noticed among the corpses evidence of a certain amount of cannibalism.

'The Nazi physicians have shown the extent of their measures to disintegrate all humanity,' she said. 'I hope that your brave brother was not one of the prisoners from Lamsdorf.'

It was she who explained to me about the electrical apparatus which was directing electricity towards my ovaries – and was very painful – and why the apathetically sad faces of thirteen hundred boys had arrived on the block. They had been brought for one reason only: the German bacteriologists wanted to sterilise them and examine the difference between the living and dead spermatozoa. When the experiments had ended the children were sent to the gas chambers.

While she was talking to me. Dr Dmitrovna felt my body for a little flesh. When she did not find any she stabbed the needle just under the skin in several places on my upper thigh: so many lumps appeared that my thigh began to resemble a rock garden!

The barrack was filled with young girls again. Dr Dmitrovna affirmed that the Bayer company had brought these two hundred girls to test their unknown products. At the same time, Dr Clauberg, the German gynaecologist, was monitoring the effects of the sterilisation experiments.

*

I hardly heard the light footsteps of the buxom SS nurse when she brought me some brown liquid to drink. I took a couple of sips of the mixture and stared at my scarred body: perspiration was running like water; the skin was yellow, shrunk like crinkled paper and bumps like minor tumours had erupted all over me. My body flushed cold and then hot during the painful process of urination. I thought that I must be experiencing a gradual invasion of death.

The myth of the Lord's Prayer entered my body: I prayed mentally so hard that my mouth was dry. At times I felt foolish to rely so much on my spiritual beliefs and yet, undoubtedly, after each prayer it seemed as though an abundance of strength and endurance was implanted in me. Gradually, I regained an unexpected degree of optimism and an overwhelming will to see my parents again. I am sure that this was the very factor which pulled me through the war.

*

The light was bayoneting my dreams when again I felt Dr Dmitrovna's gentle hand on my head. She jotted something down on my chart and then she whispered, 'You will be transferred to Dachau in a few days' time with the next transport. They may even let you work on the land!'

Oh, how I felt that tiny bit of freedom seeping into my pores, even though the chaos still remained, piled up in front of me. I could hardly remember the joy of warmth, and the flowers: it had been stamped out by the Nazis' world of tyranny – all because the Bayer pharmaceutical company, driven by monetary greed, wished to prove their worthiness to the *Führer* at the cost of thousands of lives.

After the war ended, I often heard the Germans saying, 'It was not *us* who had the concentration camps.' It was not surprising that none of them wanted to admit their responsibility. They have left their victims buried in torment. The old saying, 'Let sleeping dogs lie', is easy to say for those who cannot even imagine our agonies: the only comfort many a victim has is to recall, from time to time, the field of cruelty and the awful havoc of the past. While the existence of God was always in my mind, I found it hard to comprehend why a human should be made to suffer, only to provide a reflection of His own suffering.

*

I had, by now, forgotten how to walk, but thanks to Dr Dmitrovna was ready to return to the barrack – my prayers had been answered. She was a living example of human compassion and gambled with her own life to help others to safety, never looking for any medals.

It was with dismay that I learned after the war that such bravery and exemplary work would not have saved Dr Dmitrovna, or others like her, from *Stalin's* concentration camps in Russia. Stalin, who was by then a dictator, had stringent rules which applied to people like her, or even to myself, although we have no special political significance and were forced from our homes. In Stalin's eyes we were guilty of desertion, or of working for the enemy and thus deserved the punishment imposed on all those who were traitors.

Back in the barrack, a quick glance around me revealed unfamiliar faces, all stumbling over their pathetic scraps of belongings. I was still not very steady on my feet and was somewhat perturbed by the new strangers, until I came eventually to a corner by the door where my old friend Tonia was trying to secure a place for herself. I saw the shocked look of horror in her eyes when she looked me up and down.

Immediately, Tonia untied her small rug and took out the contents – a few crusts of bread – which she made me eat. I humbly accepted the crusts and it took only a few minutes to stow them away into my shrunken stomach.

*

I was not long back at the barrack when we were summoned, shortly before dawn, to dozens of trucks waiting by the main gate to the camp. It was the autumn of 1944 and the sirens were wailing.

I could not tell exactly how many trucks there were as I could not see where the last one ended, nor can I remember the date, or even which day of the week it was. In the midst of mounting confusion we were piled on top of each other, the SS men using their rifles to push us even more tightly into the trucks. I was pathetically happy just to pass through that evil gate. With two SS guards at the front and the rear of the truck we sped away from the sign above the gate: ironically it read: '*Arbeit macht frei*' - Work makes people free.

Despite being crushed in the truck we could still see through the parted tarpaulin. The warm red glow over the forest and the forlorn Polish houses stared at us in the vermilion dawn. The extreme warmth of the sun penetrated the earth and a slight mist rose from the valley.

During the long journey, we came to terms with accepting our impending fate in the new surroundings. I felt the presence of Tonia's comforting arm over my shoulder; it was so good to have someone from my own country beside me. It must have been a couple of months since she went to work in 'Canada', and I . . . But we could not talk about it – the SS guard saw to that. When the truck stopped sharply, we were told by the guard that we had entered Dachau Camp. We arrived at night-time and had to wait for hours for daylight.

My eyes goggled, my mouth fell open and I remained as though rooted to the ground as I scanned the horrible grey-looking buildings: everything smelt of decay. I thought for a minute that we were back in Auschwitz. The first scene which met my eyes was that of prisoners laying out the dead by each barrack: those who had died during the night had to be counted at the early roll call.

I heard some music in the background, and a huge squad of slave labourers were marched by their leader through the main gate and away to work. My natural curiosity made me walk too near the gate and I was siezed with a sudden urge to dive across it along with the work squad. With my hands outstretched, I was barely touching the gate of 'freedom' when a guttural voice reached my ears. '*Halt! Halt*!' a man was yelling, then the end of a rifle crashed heavily on my head and a second blow darted on to the front of my mouth. The most violent pain beset my body: blood squirted from my mouth and nose uncontrollably – I did not know that I had such a lot of blood left in my pitiful body.

I saw dazed figures dancing before me and tried to wipe the blood from my eyes, before I fell heavily on the rough ground. I heard the SS guard swearing and Tonia crying out; then the darkness quickly took over my mind as I lay, sprawled in a pool of blood. I was left lying there, as an exhibit to deter others, until the daylight had disappeared.

When I regained consciousness, my mouth felt numb and the two front teeth were missing, lying in the congealed blood. In a state of shock I stuck the teeth back into their places where they remained, wobbly, for many years after! With the assistance of the SS guard's bayonet at my bottom and a stern warning to stay away

75

from the gate, I got up and walked, still dizzy, to the barrack.

*

It would not take us long to find out that Dachau was much the same as Auschwitz, only on a much smaller scale. One difference I noticed was that the SS men were all much older than those in Auschwitz. I found out later that, towards the end of 1944, the younger men had been summoned to the front for active service.

The food was the same: black liquid in the morning, watery soup at lunchtime and a tiny portion of black bread was the ration for one day. Often, however, the guards would keep back the rations and sell our food on the black market, leaving us with nothing.

Of course, the SS guards in Dachau were also practising their bestialities without being reprimanded, the same as those in Auschwitz and the German soldiers who were fighting in Russia. They were all firmly protected by Hitler's assurance that no German soldier could be brought to trial for any act committed against Soviet citizens. As a result of this licence, within a few days of Hitler's rule in Kiev fifty-two thousand men, women and children had been tortured and then murdered. But Dachau had not always been a mountain of barbed wire and watchtowers. It had an honourable history prior to its days as a concentration camp. The renaissance palace of the Bavarian royal family, the Wittelsbachs, and the Church of St Jacob are witnesses today of a rich past. The well-known Bavarian author, Ludwig Thoma, regarded Dachau as his literary birthplace.

I returned to Dachau in 1975. There were busloads of American children, laughing and chattering, totally unaware of those silent murdered voices which I still felt in every crevice of the land. Almost everything had gone – transformed into parking spaces – except a plaque, one barrack and the gas chambers.

Today, the city of Dachau asks us to bear in mind that Dachau shares an equal measure of responsibility for what happened there with every other German city. Not less, but also not more.

In the victims' eyes, it is not the *cities* which are to be blamed for the terror which reigned there, but the monsters who lived in them. From the palace and other buildings, the people of Dachau were constantly witnessing hordes of nearly naked prisoners slaving in their fields from sunrise to the darkness. Who did they think we were? Slave labour from another planet? Where was their goodwill towards any one of us when they saw the guards whip our backs until we could no longer bend down? They see their memorial as a warning against the inhumanity of the Nazi system, but who were the Nazis?

It is easy to sketch and water down some of the incidents of the terror inflicted by the Nazis, especially for those writers who were fortunate enough to escape such a horror, or the German internees in the camps who were treated in a more humane manner: they had reasonable clothes to wear, food to eat and food parcels and their rooms were said to be provided with writing tables and books for them to read! Even with all this comparative luxury they would merely complain, 'We got a beating and kicking'.

While they sat and read cosily during the severe winter we were shovelling the snow all day long, wearing only light clothes. When we could no longer work from fatigue the camp kapos standing behind us would hit us with their sticks. Some of the internees had to take the snow in small barrows and carts to the nearby River Wurmbach: many of them gasped for breath under such a heavy burden, but instead of showing any caring attention the SS guards only lashed out with more kicks — knocking them down unconscious.

*

I rushed into the Russian mixed barrack. There too, several hundred heads, most of them shaven, met my eyes; a thousand eyes were staring at the open door which was bulging with the newcomers. In the middle of the foul-smelling prisoners there stood a black-haired SS man, with a whip in his hand ready to dole out the lashes. A cluster of females sat on a bunk to his left, plucking awkwardly at their lice.

'Oh God!' I exclaimed aloud. When was it going to end? I felt pain stabbing me from all directions and my stomach twitched with hunger.

Tonia and I stumbled into the crowd, hungry, ill and tired, trying to find a small corner from where we might escape the keen eye of the SS guard.

She told me how she had been sent to work at the registration section, even while I still lay bleeding. Tonia had noticed that the man who was in charge of keeping the records had been chewing something as he worked – a registration paper belonging to one of the new arrivals. She explained, almost as incredulous as I was, how, as the time drew nearer for his own execution, he was actually destroying the prisoners' records by chewing them. So much for the accuracy of the camp records!

After the war, Mama tried everything to ascertain my whereabouts. She was always told she 'is not here ... has never been here ... and is not on or files.'

I felt a gentle touch on my hand – Kera was ready to render a little kindness to a stranger. Only we were not strangers: we met in Auschwitz before our transfer. She had been a healthier being then, although not by any normal standards, but now I could hardly recognise her decaying little body. It was cruel even to look at Kera: she resembled an old lady whose body had not been given the time to develop.

She explained that she had been recently discharged from Dachau's infirmary, where she had been subjected to experiments for tropical diseases. The machinery of science wheeled fast under the Dachau scientists, who enriched their knowledge without any consideration for their subjects' suffering. The physician Dr Klaus was an expert on directing insects to bite the selected patients to stimulate the development of malaria. Kera's wounds on her arms and legs remained open and untreated; however much she was tormented by her pain there was no remedy available to treat her disease. Whenever I think of this kind of evil, even now, I am overtaken by rage, horror and confusion until I no longer know which saint to shout at. I then follow my usual path and plunge for the Nazis.

There was a Polish woman who slept in a bunk next to mine. It was obvious that her life on this earth had almost finished – she was visibly sinking. She looked seventy years old, but may only have been in her forties: she too was a victim, this time of ulceration experiments. I remember one day when I could hardly bring myself to look at her horribly ravaged face as she tried to nurse her wounds – the size of a saucer on her arms and legs – filled with bloody pus. After her leg was amputated, I could no longer ignore the distress on her exhausted face and made myself moisten her bloodless lips with black coffee, listening to her feverish lamentations about Faust and Goethe. Sadly, when I returned from work late in the evening, she had been removed without leaving a trace.

*

I spent my days labouring in the fields, as Dr Dmitrovna had indicated. The work was hard, but at least it was outside the camp. We would be taken each morning by truck to work: on the harvest, potato picking, clearing snow — we never knew from one day to the next.

I found out on my way to work how the ordinary Germans also had experienced their share of tragedy. It was one of the dullest of autumn days as the truck was speeding back to Dachau. I heard the most deafening noise, pulled the canvas back and watched the bombs falling aggressively on the stone buildings. We were just outside the Munich boundary. To my amazement, I saw an extraordinary amount of feathers released in thick clouds into the air before settling on a clump of trees which had been badly damaged by the bombs and which was laden with corpses. They were somebody's children. I loathed and abhorred Hitler, the SS and all those who made and executed the rules which terrorised our lives.

Today, as I constantly turn the pages of my life, I wonder what it would have been like to have lived with my loving family in my homeland like any other little girl — without the concentration camps, without pain and, most of all, without war.

*

In the autumn of 1944 the weather was very changeable. Allied planes were conducting mass air raids around Munich, which were welcomed passionately by the prisoners, although one or two were worried by the thought that the camp could have been reduced to rubble. It was at this point that the camp's commandant stepped up the workforce of younger prisoners in order to accelerate the harvest before the bombs could imperil the year's crops.

In the early hours of the morning, we would be summoned for our work call, only afterwards receiving our mug of brown liquid and a slice of black bread. We then marched to the waiting trucks by the gate.

The SS guards moved strangely in their sphere of power. One of these SS men, whose eyes were tempestuous in their deep yellow sockets, chose to carry out his role by hitting every prisoner with his rifle as he pushed us into the truck, fulfilling his personal sadistic desires.

The truck passed through the main gates with intense speed. My mouth ached from the previous beating and was infected. Kera's wounds were weeping. It was Tonia who remained the strongest and helped to sustain our sanity.

The trees in the distance looked like a theatre of sleeping beauties; already their tops were stained with the golden tints of autumn. We were not aware of our destination until we saw the sign for Munich. At last, the truck raced round the final bend before resting by a large wooden gate, alongside numerous other vehicles. There were hundreds of acres of land before us and the fields were full of workers from the camp, our torsos all unhealthy and our movements as though drugged with exhaustion. But the pure joy of being in the open field gave me fresh energy as I began the back-breaking task of picking potatoes – always under the watchful eyes of the SS guards.

A huge farm building was partly hidden by the trees, only a short distance from the field. The fields themselves were full of natural beauty – as lovely as the landscapes of Samuel Palmer. The birds were singing and the rabbits prancing to and fro in the leafy woodland; the wild pigeons cooing furiously, dancing and bowing on the fresh earth and radiating an infinite love for each other. The chickens were lazily pecking at the cow-dung.

I tried to satisfy my hunger pangs by eating a raw potato, which only made me violently sick and resulted in me being sent to work on another part of the field as a punishment. Still choking, I had to carry on working if I were to avoid further beating. When I eventually recovered I tried hard to find a familiar face: all around me had reached such an unrecognizable physical condition that everyone tended to look the same. It was a blessing that we had no mirrors to reveal our ugliness, or we might have died of shock.

Apart from a short break at lunchtime, we worked all day. By the time the sun had gone to rest, I was tired and my feet were bleeding; my toes peeped through the torn canvas on both my right-footed shoes. At long last, when even the SS guards could no longer watch the suffering prisoners labouring in the dark, we were summoned back to the trucks. Crammed together for the painful journey back to Dachau, we could hardly distinguish the pains in our anatomies – one part ached as bad as the other – but every one of us was determined not to give in to our bitterness.

There was very little for us to see on our return journey. The city of Munich was in total darkness apart from the searchlights and the humming aeroplanes. As soon as we reached the camp I dived for the lower corner of a bunk and fell, senseless, into a deep sleep, not stirring until the guard sounded his whistle for the next morning's work call. The same procedure continued each morning: after we had drunk the brown liquid with a small piece of bread the slaves were marched to work either on foot, or in some sort of transport.

My Mama used to tell me a sad story about the African slaves and describe how the poor things were tortured and tied in heavy chains, then sold to a big, fat, white capitalist, without recourse or litigation. But the Nazis now seemed far worse with their gas chambers, tortures and these horrid experiments.

*

Towards the end of 1944, nobody could tell what our fate would be. Machine guns were always mounted on the towers, their barrels directed constantly on to the camp; anyone who accidentally wandered off would meet with a spray of fire from the towers, without warning. Incidents frequently occurred when prisoners, in pain and despair, threw themselves against the electric fence.

I can remember one morning when the SS guards carried out a search, with their ferocious dogs, and ransacked the Czechs' block, from which several prisoners had somehow managed to get out during the night. Around nightfall, we heard a lot of shooting and an even greater number of SS guards were to be seen. We learned later that the escapees had been unable to hide and were killed near the camp, that same evening. Even though the governance had progressively relaxed under the older SS guards, they still observed their universal rules for the various classifications of selections and escapes – the punishment was death.

The autumn cold now had us in its grip and although there was no thermometer to record the temperature, I could feel the brisk air all around me as we assembled for work. The mud from the previous day was still flaking off my ragged clothing as we stood waiting, in contempt and amid the sound of many languages – without honour, without names.

The work call was interrupted by a sudden roar of aeroplanes. Never before had we been pushed so quickly into the trucks, or driven away from the camp so fast. We were heading in the same direction as where we had first worked on the potato harvest.

The bombardment had begun; the truck's windows were broken by the first blast and it swayed crudely from side to side. An avalanche of explosions burst around the whole area. Some of the prisoners who had experienced this adversity before concealed themselves in a corner; others jumped for joy. But the SS guards held on to their weapons.

We had only just reached the field where we were to work and had been detailed to clear it – the order had hardly the time to echo to the other end of the field – when the alarm sounded from the direction of Munich. It was far too late: the Allied planes hovered directly over the field. We just stood there. For us, there was no place to hide.

The SS guards panicked and ran in every direction to shelter in the thick woodland. Before running for cover, I looked up nimbly at the sky: it was crowded with aeroplanes heading for Munich and the *Messerschmitts* were only metres away. Suddenly, the world darkened.

CHAPTER FOUR

ESCAPE FROM DACHAU

Behind the curtain of smoke, the sky had turned into a red inferno: the bombs were falling like raindrops. The anti-aircraft defences did all that they could to ward off their enemy's planes, but the Allies would have none of it and continued to unload their bombs. Just as we reached the conifer-clad woodland, a *Messerschmitt* and a white-starred Allied plane tumbled down, tangled with each other, and set the field on fire.

Tonia and Kera were close beside me, amongst the twigs, leaves and long grass behind the rotten wattle fence which surrounded the field. We dare not even pant aloud in case the SS guards were near by. Cautiously, we moved further and further into the woods, most of the time on our bellies. When I caught my first glimpse of the sky, through a gap in the trees, the planes were waltzing in the air, ammunition exploding up above and a most awful deafening noise below.

It had suddenly become a scene of pandemonium: the field we had left behind was full of prisoners, screaming and struggling against the SS guards. I was very frightened, but concealed my fear from my two friends. I could not help but worry about our chances of survival without food, adequate clothing or compass. At least a compass would have been able to tell us where on earth we were, as it had when I last used it at my school camp.

For days, we wandered through the forest, hiding in the undergrowth. We picked blackberries to eat, slept amongst dry leaves and in the morning we washed our faces with the dew. How can I put into words the kind of joy, the sense of freedom and perfect peace we gained, even if just for a few days?

It took us a long time to pick the mud off our clothes and we combed our hair with our hands as best we could. We were burning with one mad ambition and one overwhelming aim – to get back to Russia. Somehow, we had chosen the hardest way, we thought, but perhaps also the cleverest of them all: as long as we could eat berries and the warm weather continued, we could hide until the war ended. The proximity of war became more apparent. Practically every day the sound of sirens frequently broke through the silence.

We rambled through the woods using as our only guide the occasional sounds of a train. The day had begun to seem darker and the mist thickly covered the uppermost part of the forest – it was like being in another planet. We heard the sound of German voices and motorbikes touring around the woods. I was petrified and started to shiver beyond all reasonable control until Kera slapped my face, and my Mama's voice managed to reach my ears as though by some supernatural force.

It had been another fruitless day. I was sure that the guards would find us if we moved from our spot. I had a kind of superstitious fear that if we moved too far from this area only disaster would follow.

We had been filled with a false delirium of freedom and were now fraught with stress from the constant bombardment and totally at a loss as to which path to follow. There was another worry too, about our 'identity' – who on earth should we say we were? The truth would only result in our being sent back to the camp. Even more important still, who *was* I? Ever since that time I have been searching for my identity without finding it – if I did find it, would it make any difference to my life?

But we had to go somewhere. We emerged from the woods and immediately stumbled on a dead SS guard, his body festering and covered with flies. Tonia's face was white, translucent with worry.

'Do you hear the clatter of a train?' Her voice was flat, but positive. We did not know which areas would be searched for the dead man, so we ran towards the sound of the train. When we could no longer run we came to rest in the tall grass, remaining there until dark.

The stabbing hunger pains had swamped me and left me lame again, forcing me to scramble down the slope, from where I grabbed a large piece off one of the greenest branches. Like irritated vultures with long beaks, we ate the leaves until the branch was completely bare.

This time it was I who heard the sound of a train and we quickly made a dash towards the long bend. Sure enough, on the little slope below, there it was – a dirty goods train, building up its steam and ready to move off into the darkness. There was still time for us to rustle a few green branches together with which to cover ourselves before we nestled unobtrusively on the buffers, completely hidden and vaguely surprised at what we had done.

Soon we were off. The train accelerated noisily towards its

destination. I wished that we knew where we were going, but we did not and our future still looked uncompromisingly grim.

We did not fall off, but the heavy rain throughout the night nearly washed us off! Kera was puffing, clinging to the slippery goods car and watching my failing efforts. Oh, how she cursed the bloody Germans!

'I simply hate the buggers for ruining our lives,' she cried.

We passed through a tunnel and when we came out the sunlight was flickering through the forest. The train once paused at a marshalling junction and I looked for the signpost: but there was none to be seen.

By the time the train came to a halt we had even eaten the limp leaves off our branches. When we eventually climbed down we carried the bare branches with us, pretending that we were picking the debris off the platform.

Vienna station was grey, full of dust, and the sky was lit up with a red glow where parts of the city still burned after the bombing. No one could deny the evidence of war, even here.

It came as a surprise to us too, that the Germans were so stricken with their own sorrow and the added peril threatening their superior race that no one paid the slightest attention to us.

Hitler's war-time Vienna had a battered look about its drab, grey buildings: it was not the fairy story of the gay waltzing city that I read about in my school books. We had never seen such emotional displays amongst the Germans – for the Austrians *were* German to us. That same nation which was causing such painful deaths to millions of prisoners was now itself being punished: a grey-headed man was sitting on a bench crying aloud; quarrelling couples were everywhere and children screaming under the falling debris.

It was not easy for us to fend for ourselves, even after our escape from Dachau camp. I felt that it was our honest-looking faces, our children's boldness and the startled wonder at being alive that got us through the rest of the war.

The city was crowded with refugees, many of them survivors of the slave labour camps like ourselves. Mama had told me many times that if I ever needed to ask for help, I must look for the person with the kindest face – who would look me straight in the eyes – and I should come to no harm. I approached an elderly nun in a crowded coffee bar and asked her if she had any food for us. She looked at us, knowingly, and then guided us to a refugee shelter situated in a bombed-out building in the city. We were even able to have a bath there: afterwards, we felt as though we had been cleansed of all the Nazis' evil . . .

From then onwards we remained at the shelter. By day, we would wander over the ruins, looking for any kind of work we could do in exchange for a few crumbs of food. But it was almost impossible to find anything, especially for refugees like ourselves. At times, though, we returned well pleased with our early morning's scavenging.

By night, the floor of the shelter would be littered with old rags and sleeping bodies. We never really got to know the people in the shelter because they were constantly moving on and no one knew who would be coming in next. The incessant cries of hungry children would break through the stale infected air of the ruin, only to be answered by the nun's tired voice: 'No food . . .'

Frequently, the nun brought to the shelter a pile of sewing and darning, with which we could help her in return for some food. By the time the work was done my fingers would be numb and bleeding with the constant pricks from the needle.

As I was nursing my painful hands one night, the nun, who had a little twist to her dehydrated mouth, came to rest beside me after her long day's work at the hospital. By this time of the night I had no energy left: I felt withdrawn, and betrayed by God. Still, I managed to smile. The nun began to speak, lifelessly, in her Yugoslavian tongue: 'Happiness is something children believe in. But those of us who have lived . . . know its unreality.'

*

The late autumn was suddenly replaced by the winter cold. The monotonous drone of sirens and the bright searchlights in the sky had become a part of our daily life. Often the clouds stood motionless. When the sound of guns came nearer, the shelter would fall into darkness; if the damage was not too great the lights would come back on the next day, but at times we went for days with no light at all.

It was nearly Christmas when the snowflakes began to fall. One evening, Kera brought a tiny Christmas tree into the shelter. It was more like a big twig, but she had worked the whole week for it! It was the first Christmas we had spent out of the camps – and what a touching time it was when all of us were gathered around the tiny tree and the strains of *Silent Night* echoed sadly throughout the shelter. We had forgotten, only momentarily, the more bestial face of Germany. I remember our Christmas meal – a small cup of some left-over soup which the nun had brought from the hospital.

Shortly after the new year, the nun called us over and gave us each an identity card, with our names and nationality altered from our own to Yugoslavian. We were told to say to anyone who asked that we had been brought to work within the hospital compound here in Austria. Of course, we had never been inside an Austrian hospital or any other for that matter, but that did not make the card any less precious. Caressing my unexpected gift, I slipped it into my pocket and kissed the nun's ageing hand in appreciation.

*

By the time Spring arrived, it hardly seemed real that we were *still* free, although often hungry. Whenever I felt hungry I thought of the many exquisite dishes that Mama had prepared before the German occupation: my nostrils smelled the tasty Chicken Kiev, dipped in herbs and garlic, and my lips felt the sweet juice of water melon.

Our dreary daily conversation would be about our earthly possessions, of which we had none, and about our daily food, for which we were at the mercy of others' benevolence. On occasions, we went to the small vegetable market and begged for food. In return, we would wash the dirty stands and then collect all the debris. We never attempted to steal, for extreme fear of being sent back to Dachau camp. Hitler's *Jugend* always had a keen eye for pointing out any faults, as they marched arrogantly through the streets, under a forest of banners.

I would ponder with a heavy heart over my unjust predicament: the only reassuring element in my mind was that the war, it seemed, was nearing its end and that soon I may find my way home again. But how? And by what means of transport? I dared not even think about such problems until the time came. Such tragic separation as mine had been was still too close to my heart, so that even these thoughts were too painful for me to bear. I could only rejoice in spirit, at the hope that some of my family may yet have survived Hitler's terror – unlike little Berta whose parents perished in the gas chambers of Dachau.

Berta was a Jewish girl who shared our shelter. Because of the increasing restlessness of the German military in the city, she had been told not to go out on the street. This virtual imprisonment had caused the eleven-year-old to chant interminably. She frequently would flap her long silky eyelashes and loudly hum an unstructured Yiddish rhapsody. During those difficult times, in the omnipresence of war, we cared for each other most deeply and developed a tremendous comradeship with even the strangers among us, which rarely exists nowadays.

The nun decided one day to take Kera and Tonia to help her with some of the hospital work, now that there were not too many officials around. Oh, how happy poor Kera was about this chance; she thought she might even be able to obtain some medicine to treat her own, still open, wounds. True enough, two weeks later the wounds were beginning to heal and new skin to form: we were all so happy for her.

Berta and I always waited patiently for Kera and Tonia to return from their hard day's work: we got some scraps of food which they concealed in their pockets together with a little milk in discarded medicine bottles.

*

Although we were contented in our temporary refuge, after a time we began to sense that something in the atmosphere was not right, and the nun looked as though she was fighting off despair.

It was a Monday evening and Kera and Tonia were at he hospital. The first drop of that evening's bombs shook the refuge into darkness yet again. The sirens were wailing but the warning had come far too late for anyone to reach safety. I heard a sudden gasp of '*Oh Gott*!' and then everybody started to rush from the bombed basement, crashing into each other in the narrow doorway. I simply froze once outside the refuge, unable to move from fright. It was horrific. I smelled the dust from the bombed buildings and felt the heat from the flames which were leaping from all directions. The bright flashes from the burning buildings had transformed the night into daylight. People were running for safety — but there was none to be found in the central vicinity.

As I stood, trembling, I felt God's presence and a total awareness of the twentieth-century misery of war. I closed my eyes, leaning against the concrete steps, and listened to the pleas for help — voices of all different intonations.

Bereft of all pity, I shouted to God, 'What are you doing to us, dear Lord? All this butchery, death, destruction, misery and sufferings ... Why? ... Why? Is this the accomplishment of our Christian teachings?'

Like my thoughts the gusts of wind blew from the river Danube and with them came the rustling bombs in their hundreds, crushing the symmetrical architecture to the ground like mashed potatoes. There was no doubt in my mind that the war was getting much tougher and there was no longer any place in which we could hide.

My eyes were fixed on the two figures approaching me. I thought that I was dreaming as I was covered in rubble and coughing up the dust which choked my lungs. But it was not a dream; it *was* Tonia and the nun. I was so happy to see them: with my arms outstretched, I touched their faces. My hands were covered in blood, but they too were hurt from the falling debris when they had been caught in a torrent of bombs only a short distance away from our refuge.

Through her sobs Tonia babbled out the news that Kera had been killed as she was running for shelter.

I gasped aloud but could not comprehend what she had told me. Taut with apprehension, I began to scream. At least, I thought, when I had calmed down, Kera was finally resting in peace and I wondered what would now become of Tonia and myself.

Tonia had hardly had time to clean the blood off her face and clothes when the nun called us sharply to her side. I noticed almost straight away two tiny bundles on a bench by the bombed stone wall. I felt deeply within me that there was something wrong ... And there was no one left in the shelter. Hurriedly, we were told that there would be raids shortly. She did not fear the bombs, but the Gestapo. 'You would be much better off if you try to reach the Italian border,' she advised. 'There will be less of them there than in the centre of Vienna.' We were to take the train which was shortly due to leave for Italy.

*

The Spring was enlivened by a sudden burst of warmth. Our life was once again entering into a new phase. All our hopes of going home had to be put aside. We had suffered cruelly, but happily had the mentality to bounce back and keep trying.

The central station in Vienna was crowded with Cossacks in German uniform; Ukrainian and Russian tongues greeted our ears as soon as we arrived on the platform. No one seemed to know which train to take, but we plunged for one which displayed a Red Cross emblem on its first few carriages. We had not quite reached the last empty carriage when an announcement came over the air informing us that some two hundred and fifty American bombers were approaching Vienna. The most awful panic that I have ever seen now broke out.

The deafening sirens continued, ceaselessly, and everyone rushed for moving trains. Women with children, clutching on to their belongings, got stuck on the railway lines: some lost their shoes in between the tracks and had to run with their bare feet. The old wreck of a train squeaked and groaned like an old man as it jerked furiously away from the station.

The sky was covered with Allied aeroplanes orbiting round the whole area. The noise was unbearable.

The train gave another harsh jerk and then raced along the rusty rails. We were thrown from side to side of the long corridor and there we remained as the enormous locomotive moved forward, snorting with its long carriages trailing behind.

The passengers were of mixed nationality, but strangely enough the predominant language was Italian, followed closely by Slavonic tongues. We could see that some of the occupants were wounded and others were foreign workers returning to Italy. There were also a few middle-aged women who had Red Cross bands on their arms, acting as first-aid attendants.

Suddenly, the mighty German artillery furiously began to pound at the Allied planes as they unleashed their bombardment on an unprecedented scale. The result on our transport was disastrous. The train was travelling too slowly to be able to reach any shelter and it simply ploughed through the exploding shells with its engine blaring. Before long, a mass of metal debris engulfed its rear carriages. Inevitably, the passengers' continental emotions were stirring.

For a long time I could not see the sky: it was obscured by the bombers in tight formation and then, with an unmistakable and authoritative sweep, they sent their bombs tumbling down on top of us. Hell had erupted.

The train came to a halt: all those passengers who were mobile slithered on their bellies to shelter underneath the carriages. Just as my turn came to jump off the step an enormous explosion flashed in front of my vision. An excruciating pain travelled through the whole of the left side of my body as I was thrown down to the ground, several metres away from the train. A cloudburst of blood stained the railway lines as far as my eyes could see. The wounded moaned, dazed and much preoccupied with the impact of the dead. The single thought which concerned me was that I might die without my true identity attached to my person: perhaps some kind person would eventually have sent it to my Mama. At least she would have been happier knowing where I was killed.

I could hear noises, but was afraid to move and just let my thoughts wander aimlessly. How much more would I have preferred to die amongst my own people in my homeland! A wave of nostalgic affection and an acute longing for Mama flooded my mind until, at last, the tangle between the *Messerschmitts* and the Allied planes finally subsided.

Much unprintable language was being expressed – in all tongues – and amongst it I heard Tonia's voice calling my name as she darted across the railway lines towards me.

'Thank God,' she uttered. I was covered in blood and a small chunk of dark-grey metal was embedded in my left hip. Tonia bent down beside me and her face twitched a little as she placed her hands firmly on the shrapnel and quickly yanked it out. Much of what happened afterwards, I do not remember.

I found myself staring at the shadows in a darkened corridor: Tonia was smiling by my side, and the repaired train was on the move. It was really wonderful how my body readjusted, dispersing its healing powers over the wounds without the help of surgery or medicine. Indeed I was amazed how my body could absorb so much punishment and yet ... I was still on my feet – ever able to help other people with their problems.

After all that had happened Tonia and I did not think much of the nun, and her advice to us. It seemed obvious that she had felt no great concern for us or she would never have sent us on this journey in which we faced a mass of mortal danger every inch of the way.

The train had, by now, approached the border of yet another strange country. We were surrounded by endless mountain peaks. My first contact with the mountains was quite unforgettable: I had never seen anything so expressive, and so alive under the blue sky. It was only when I came to Scotland that I found mountains even more profoundly beautiful: surrounded by their lochs and waters as blue as the Mediterranean.

I was sitting by a broken window, still in pain, and I gulped a breath of scented mountain air just before an exploding shell on the track brought the train to a standstill. I could also see smouldering fires all over the area. One sheer hell of a panic broke out during the pandemic air attack which followed: in a matter of seconds it seemed as though we had reached the end of the world. Everything went dark.

Those who were able to run trampled over us as if we were stepping stones. The train's engine roared, but the wheels were not moving. Tonia and I held on to the wood by the broken window, beside an elderly man who had collapsed on his mangled legs. His eyes were closed and the pain was strangling his breath, but he remained perfectly aware of the shelling. He tried to speak, but his mouth was crusted with blisters.

When one of the wagons exploded into a blazing inferno I thought that we were really finished. By this point Tonia had dragged me along almost to the last compartment and, without consciously thinking about what we were doing, we eased ourselves into a wilderness of undergrowth. For some time, we hid under a large protruding rock until the daylight had disappeared. By the time we emerged from our hiding place, hungry, cold and tear-stained, there was no sign of the train. We had been left behind – in a scenario of bewilderment and horror.

That night we again slept under the rock. Although we had very little knowledge about botany, we came to no harm as a result of eating various mountain plants. The mountains reverberated with ceaseless echoes of gunfire, bombing or distant shouts. It was only later that I learned that the Germans were at that time retreating towards Austria, blasting their guns at the Italian partisans who were entrenched deep within the Alps.

Early next morning, when the mist had disappeared and the blazing sun lit up the world once more, we decided to walk the short distance towards the town or village we could see. That walk was like a journey between heaven and hell!

We tried to run but I was still losing blood and kept falling down. The guns were firing from the mountains and exploding shells fell in our path, only a few metres in front of us. The roaring aircraft overhead polluted the beautiful blue sky with their smoke-screens. We crawled on our stomachs for the best part of the way and only when the attack had subsided did we get up to stretch our hungry bodies.

I closed my eyes and began to pray. I noticed that Tonia had sunk wearily back into her own private struggles with the pain from the shredded skin on her belly – a result of our crawling. Her pale, injured flesh was red and angry, and in need of cleansing, but we could not find any water with which to clean it until eventually we reached the Italian border village.

*

In the narrow square the inhabitants were all talking excitably together, gathered around the carts and watching the ugly presence of the German tanks which roamed the dusty narrow streets. Underneath the window of a white-washed house, a brown-haired cat nestled in a flower box, pawing happily with the red geraniums and quite unaware of the grim reality engulfing his birthplace.

Our dirty clothes and ruffled appearance blended in well amongst the natives: at this stage in the war the Germans had no time for specific distinctions as they were too preoccupied with retreating as fast as they could.

It was a joy to see the farm animals again – a touching reminder of my home. There were even some houses which resembled those I had known and loved. Chickens and rabbits were frantically running about the square, darting in front of the carts; the low-flying aircraft stirred the green leaves which clad the branches of the tall trees. If only for a moment, I almost forgot the bestiality of war.

CHAPTER FIVE

THE WAR IS OVER

Inside the white-washed house, by an open window, there stood a kindly-faced woman of large frame and sallow skin, with dancing black eyes which were permanently smiling. She was not young but it was difficult to tell what her age might have been. We thought that she must be religious as she held a cross restlessly in her hand.

She detected our hardship immediately and came out to greet us with a large white china jug of water, cheerfully waving the jug in the air with the words: '*Aqua, aqua! Prego, prego bambine*'. We almost ran into this strange woman's arms as though she was our own Mama . . .

After we had drunk the water, she ushered us into the house and waved us into the kitchen. A few moments later, an old, bearded man appeared by the kitchen table and harshly slapped the woman's bottom. She jumped briskly and they both collapsed into loud laughter. Roughly, he wiped his face with both hands and then lifted a large green bottle of wine from off the shelf and stuck the neck of the bottle into his mouth: the wine ran all over his chest.

He chanted, '*Salute! Salute a la vittoria!*' The poor man tried very hard to make us understand that the war was coming to an end, but we could not understand him. However, we did finally make out his meaning from a combination of sign language and his expression as he said, '*bang, bang finito*'.

The fighting was at an end! It was difficult for us to understand the Italian language since we had not been taught it at school, but a little Latin made all the difference, as well as the friendly atmosphere. We understood that we were to stay with the Pedros (as we called them) until the road over the mountains was less congested with Germans and partisans. Mrs Pedro looked towards the door with a curious smoothness in her expression and the blood ran to her cheeks as her words tumbled out. We could only communicate in sign language. Mr Pedro's dark eyes were full of tolerance – his hands held an infinite vocabulary of meaning – and from time to time he exposed a mouth of rotten teeth.

We sat down at the bare wooden table to share their delicious smelling meal . . . We had not seen a table like that since our days at home – laden with a big bowl of pasta, bread and onions – a feast fit for a king! Those humble people were so friendly and they fussed over us as though they had known us for a lifetime. Tonia and I had forgotten how to laugh, but Mr Pedro made such an effort to amuse us with his various facial contortions that soon we could not help ourselves.

From where I was sitting, I noticed that the war had condemned the houses to fall into an almost primitive state of decay: the green mould and musty smell remind me now of seaweed, on the cold shores of the North Sea. There were no buildings visible at all higher up in the mountains, only yellow-stained paths which seemed to zig-zag endlessly towards the peaks and beautiful green, virgin fields warming themselves, silently tuneless, in the sun.

But the very air around us still trembled with the sound of warfare. In the dusty street which wound outside the Pedro's small house, there were scores of peasants, with children clinging tightly to their little bundles, led by a bearded little man dressed in a green uniform. The uniform conveyed nothing to Tonia and myself: it was their bare feet that reminded me of Auschwitz. The women had their heads covered with squares of dull coloured fabric, and their faces reflected much sorrow.

'Santa Maria,' exclaimed Mr Pedro, 'all these people are German slaves . . .'

He waved his hands above his head, scratching his thick growth of hair, and tears flowed along his cheeks like a stream flowing down from a steep mountain. He was overcome by the mutilated scene, but unable to articulate his voice of protest.

How clearly I remember the words of one of the kapos in Dachau who told us that the German nation believes that life has been created for only one specific type of human amidst all the innumerable sort of insects. That specific type is undoubtedly German – all others to the German eyes, are nothing but vermin. We have to train them for our use . . . and for those of you who fail – there is another place . . .

His deep, bass voice, full of supremacy and laughter, had filled my ears then and it haunts me even now . . .

*

A nagging anxiety was implanted inside me: I felt anew the despair and agony of wanting the war to end – an end to all the human beings being mutilated, so that we could let all the children grow, and the birds sing in their natural habitat.

Abruptly, the church bells began to ring an uneven tune. I went outside, feeling sleepy, for a breath of fresh air. This drowsy little place which had offered us shelter and friendship was almost destroyed by the war, and yet I felt exhilarated as I drank in the cool mountain sunlight which sprang towards me from behind a dazzling rainbow.

Tonia came out to me and we stood, under the overhanging eaves of the house, looking together at the green Alps sloping gently towards the village. We wondered which road would take us over the mountains and back to Austria . . .

*

Mr Pedro nervously held yet another huge bottle of wine in his mouth and the front of his shirt was saturated with the red liquid. Each time he swallowed some wine his lips trembled as he spat on the damp earth, watching the mass of Germans retreating.

I call the family 'Pedro' because at the time I did not really know their correct name: in war, one did not have to know people intimately to form a tower of strength and comradeship. But this kind of friendship was to become less prevalent as the new generation invaded the world – the generation who never felt pain, hunger or the trembling of limbs from the terror around them. What can they tell us except that this selfish new world belongs to them?

After the blazing sun of the morning, the rain came bucketing down. I brushed the raindrops off my face and listened to the roaring thunder overhead. The church bells rang instinctively faster to sound the alarm, but the Allied planes were already flying low over the village. The innocent-looking machines dominated the sky, glistening as they wove between the clouds which ranged from darkest grey to fluffy white, overhead. I could hardly believe that at any moment the planes might release their lethal weapons over this densely crowded village.

Before that thought had even left my mind the first bomb shook the Pedro's home, and the shutters were flung from the windows and on to the square. Several strangers ran excitedly to join us in the darkness of the house. Only one tiny beam of light crept in through a small air-vent. It sounded as though quite a large crowd of Italians with their young children were now with us. Unmoving shadows in the darkness. Piercing, unendurable screams came from the children and prayers from the adults. We heard the planes circle around once more and then ... one almighty explosion which crushed part of the building above us: we were buried beneath the rubble.

Very little oxygen now came through the vent which had become blocked. Our panic increased in such a confined space, and we choked with the dust which was swirling everywhere, like an ominous storm.

A long time had passed, but no one came near us. We could still hear the bombers' reckless activities and were dimly aware of the peril we were in. But there was even a greater danger immediately above us, where a huge support beam had parted from the main structure of the building and was creaking with the most penetrating sounds as it swayed further from the ceiling. Some of the stronger people among us stood with their hands tightly jammed against the beam, while the rest of us tore with our bare hands, at the earth and stones blocking the vent, until it collapsed inwards.

Our cries for help were useless, until the bombers had at last completed their mission. Eventually, we crawled out, one by one, into the pitch blackness of the night. The square was full of shadows but without a trace of guttural voices. The Germans had all gone.

For the remainder of the night we rested with many others by the church; we were terribly scared. Even the moon was hidden that night in a stream of clouds.

We were piled together in rows: some of us slept in a sitting position, others were chatting, but Tonia and I were wrapped in our own bitter thoughts until the early dusk.

When the light returned Tonia went off and disappeared from my sight for a little while. She returned later, clapping her hands with joy and rushed to embrace me. Through her excitement she said, 'I found a really wide road and lots of automobiles there too. But *no Germans*.' We were jumping in the air at the prospect of progressing nearer our homeland.

She stood on her toes and pointed: 'There ... and a little higher and we'll be over the pass.'

'Oh yes. But what's on the other side of the pass?' I asked.

'Well, like Mr Pedro told us ... some heavenly valleys, towns and open roads for us to go home. It's like going to a new planet for us.'

I felt a curtain of freedom drape itself over me: but it was impossible to come to terms with the idea that there would be no more Germans to practise their cruel tactics again.

We passed Mr Pedro, whose shirt was soaked in sweat as he cleared the rubble from his bomb-damaged building: methodically he set the best stones to one side and put the chips into a rust-riddled barrow. The cat was excited for some reason, jumping about and then squatting on the heap of stones.

An old lady, who was dressed to her ankles in black, her face wrinkled with hundreds of tiny lines, kindly offered us as much milk as we could drink from a galvanised metal pail sitting by her side. We drank the milk, kissed the lady's dainty hand for her kindness and then we were on our way.

In wartime everything happens so quickly, that there is never much time left for partings: we were always in a hurry to hide from the Germans, the bombs or the machine guns. It is because of this and because of my distorted youth that some parts of my life only come back to me as if through a dim haze of clouds.

*

As I focused my eyes on the mountain's high peak — so high that even the birds could not reach it — I wondered what chance we would have of managing to walk over it to the other side. My dark brown stockings were in shreds, my shoes worn thin and their heels had long ago been lost. Tonia's garments — what was left of them — were just as bad, but we were not ashamed of our appearance, just as long as our *minds* could withstand the torment we felt and dwell only on the promise of goodness to come.

We often would wonder why it was that when we prayed for God's guidance we still often came up against many obstacles and inexhaustable depths of evil which in the end had only perpetuated the hatred in our hearts.

How very wrong I was to believe that God would punish the guilty Nazis. Over the years since the war ex-SS men and Nazis have been found to be participating in the German government at the highest level, while their victims were still nursing their grotesque physical and phsychological wounds. What kind of compassion could a victim dare to hope for from a German government minister who might have to resign from his post because of his strong Nazi connections?

*

We had just reached the end of the square, as we set off towards the mountains, when we heard shouts of '*Bravo! Bravo!*' The people of the village slapped their outstretched hands along the first batch of slow-moving tanks and nearly pulled some of the soldiers down to the ground. Behind the tanks there followed the military trucks, jammed with fighting men. Some of them jumped off the vehicles, embracing the young and the old. We were too ignorant to recognise the difference in their military uniforms: they could have come from space for all we cared, as long as they left us alone.

The whole village had turned into a happy carnival, devoid of its former fear. Tonia and I kept walking, gazing meanwhile at the excited new soldiers who seemed to shift uneasily through the friendly people like a volcanic flow.

It would have been foolish to expect that I could overcome my pain and relax my violent struggle for survival simply because the shooting had died down. It was not easy to understand the world as I saw it – full of the silence of drowned sleepers, occasionally interrupted by the intolerable sound of weeping.

We were curiously absorbed in the strange military figures which reminded me, somehow, of equestrian statues – so smart in their khaki uniforms. I was still tormented by pain and the swelling in my joints and as the figures came nearer displaying their (as we later discovered) American and British flags, I thought that my eyes must be playing tricks. Throughout that splendid historical hour in my life a gentle image of Kera's face appeared clearly before me – laughing and crying in those other, gruesome days, clasping myself and Tonia by her side and watching with compassion the tumultuous excitement in this friendly place.

She loved all human beings and spent many hours by our side: we had talked mostly of those millions of things we recalled from our childhood in Russia and only then of our existence in the Nazis' hands, frequently with tearful eyes and halting words. A sphere of light illuminated my vision of Kera's face – she would have been so happy to have seen the Liberation, and the joy without affliction.

On 29 April 1945 the gates of Dachau were opened to freedom by the American liberators. While our friends in the camp were declaring us dead, we enjoyed a splendid celebration with cooked goulash!

For us the war had ended.

*

We found ourselves on the road over the Alps, lost in the vortex of thousands of refugees who were heading in the same direction. The wandering civilians were so numerous that they congested the wide road until it became no more than a narrow path. Women, it seemed, outnumbered the men: each and every one of them following their own destination. Several elderly women were pushing large perambulators, packed tightly with possessions but empty of any babies. Many refugees were celebrating in a cheerful uproar; others sat in silence by the roadside and watched the constant stream of military convoys with tired eyes.

We climbed towards the Austrian border and our feet became progressively more swollen; we were hungry, tired and destitute – high up in the Alps. The cool air was beating around our bodies in the starless night and only the smell of grass and the sound of voices calling up and down the road made us sometimes remember where we were.

The dawn silence and desolation was dispelled by the British military trucks' flickering lights on the temporary refuges erected by the roadside: their occupants were soon on the move again. Tonia and I found a cluster of women and children brewing tea by a small bonfire and went to join them. We were all amazed by the soldiers' generosity when they distributed even the tiniest portion of chocolate amongst us children and the grey-headed grandpa, who was almost hidden by the woman in front of him, received a little tobacco to roll himself a cigarette.

We exchanged our names, but were extremely sceptical about telling strangers about our birthplace. In turn, they told us that they came from the area near Rostov on Don, but it is doubtful whether they revealed their true identity. I could sense an atmosphere of mistrust as though a trial awaited them, and they proceeded always with caution.

The daylight slipped away behind the mountains so quickly that we continued walking with our companions late into the night, until we fell where we stood. Everything was damp from the mist and not even a small corner remained dry enough in which to shelter.

With a few other eight and ten-year-old children, we went up into a woody area to find some dead wood to keep the bonfire going. After an hour or so, I felt the rain-laden clouds against my face. The scavenging came to an end when the rain came down in torrents: it was like being caught on a ship-wreck in the middle of a tempest. By the time we arrived back at the roadside with the rain-drenched wood, the party had spread a canvas sheet over the perambulators under which we could sit and we managed to dry our clothes by the flickering fire.

The following morning, Tonia and I awoke to terrible confusion: we were left by the roadside and our acquaintances had gone.

My legs could not carry me any further; my feet were so swollen that now even what remained of my footwear could not be made to fit. We remained by the roadside for many hours. People passed us constantly, as if they had not seen our suffering. But we had become accustomed to this way of living – outside, without money, food or protective clothing. After all, it was God's will to either let us survive or die: these things are in His hands.

By that time we were well able to blend ourselves into any shade of background and had no difficulty either in communicating with any stranger we might meet. We waited for something to happen until late in the afternoon. Suddenly we noticed that a horse-driven cart was heading our way. Its owner had a powerful, skeletal chest and raged ceaselessly in Polish at the harnessed animals. We called out to him, and he pointed for us to climb on the cart. But our poor appearance disturbed the look on the man's face, and with a shower of affectionate greetings he reached down and helped to hoist me on the cart.

We slid into the wooden cart like two slippery eels and lay on top of some heavy bundles at the back. There were two rusty rifles tied on to the side and two pots and a water container tied to the front with a rope. The adventurous, and rather grand, old man's grey hair was flowing in the mountain breeze as he drove the cart steadily, as he would a locomotive. At one stage he put his right hand on his chest and said, 'Ja, Josef Dabrowski. To you I am Josef.'

We tried hard to express our fondest gratitude to him, but Josef just waved his hands, still holding on to the harness.

Tonia positioned her body on top of a frail bundle: it split and several books fell out, the pages shifting gently in the wind. A volume, in Polish, of Voltaire, which was badly stained but readable, fell on to my lap — the French philosopher's interpretation of Newton's principle which seemed to have a lot to do with a falling apple! While I was in paradise with the apples, Tonia went into the mythical world of Droste's *Die Judenbuche*: it had been a long time since we had seen such books. Eagerly we scoured the creative literary works, expressing our respect and admiration for the gifted writers. Tonia did not care much for Droste, especially for the matter concerning the murder of the Jew Aaron, and she had promptly changed it for Emile Zola. 'We have seen enough in Auschwitz,' she added.

'Jews? Auschwitz?' The old man's face softened as he began to speak in a reasonably good German tongue. All at once he poured out his personal tragic story. How the Gestapo had stormed into his home in Warsaw for no reason: they had arrested his wife Ada with their eleven-year-old son Saul, while he had escaped by the rear window. Josef had not heard of them since, but he was going to search for them now that the war was over.

When Tonia mentioned the name of Adolf Hitler it was like venom to him: the veins in his temples were swollen with anger. He fumbled in the breast pocket of his olive-green corduroy jacket and pulled out a crumpled map of the world, on which the clearly coloured boot of Italy was well behind us. By the time he had cursed Hitler and pointed out his native country of Poland, his anger had left him.

Josef had an educated mind and his warmth showed itself in all our conversations: his knowledge of literary works flowed from his mouth like a fountain. But now he told us, with a cold calmness in his voice, of Hitler's death, and swore that his evil judges would themselves be judged by their prisoners. Tonia and I were jumping for joy at the news.

Of course, the Nazi murderers have since been tried — at the Nuremberg Trials — but only a few of those war criminals were sentenced to death: many of those remaining are still alive today. Why should I care? As long as I was away from the raging torrent of the Nazis' misanthropy. What did the Western judges care about the whole villages which were murdered in Russia and Czechoslovakia? And, indeed, what did the Western judges care about the Czechoslovakian village which was even erased from the records? The male adults were shot; the women were sent to concentration camps and the children separated from mothers and sent to a concentration camp at Gneisenau – they have not been seen again. The very young babies were all taken to the German hospital in Prague for examination to determine if they were suitable for absorption into the Nazi master race and fitted the Aryan standards for adoption into German families. All trace of them has been lost. The rest – those who failed the test – were sent into the gas chambers in Treblinka.

In 1942 the German district commissioner near Kiev reported his personal activities to the minister, Alfred Rosenberg:

> In August 1942 measures had been taken against two families each of which was to supply one slave labour recruit. Both had been requested but did not come. They had to be brought by force, but, they succeeded twice in escaping from the collecting camp in Kiev. Before the second arrest, the fathers of both workers were taken into custody as hostages, to be released only when their sons appeared. I then decided at last to take steps to show the increasingly rebellious Ukrainian youth that our orders must be obeyed. I ordered the burning of the houses of the two refugees.

After Rosenberg's own capture, cuttings taken by the Nazis' censors from letters written by the Russians were found in his files. One of these read:

> They have already been hunting here for a week and have not got enough. The imprisoned workers were locked in the school house, they cannot even perform their natural functions, and have to do it like pigs in the same room. People from many villages went the other day on pilgrimage to Paszajaw monastery – they were all arrested and will be sent away to work. Amongst them are cripples, the blind and the aged. Russian children were used as live targets for the musketry training of the Hitler *Jugend.* When the German troops arrived near Smolensk – they shot 200 school children, boys and girls who were in the field helping with the harvest. At Kiev, the capital of the Ukraine, within a few days of its capture, fifty two thousand men, women and children were tortured and murdered.

It was just as well that I was only a schoolgirl while this was happening and failed to fully understand the reality of such brutalities – or perhaps I too may not have survived to hear the news of Hitler's death!

*

Josef fumbled inside one of the bundles and his chubby hands pulled out a long piece of rope with which to repair the wheel he had just retrieved from some fifty metres down the slope. The metal part around the wood had split and it threatened to cause a major calamity.

It was the beginning of a new and beautiful day, and since we were not very far from the border, Tonia and I decided to go on alone, leaving Josef to get on with the repair. We embraced and said our farewells to Josef, who promised to catch up with us at the first Austrian town. Genuine tears appeared in his eyes when he handed us a small jute bag containing a few provisions; he then bent down and tied my left shoe together with another piece of jute cloth. With his warmth, humanity and tacit recognition of our children's desperation – with true paternal care – he patted us on the head and said, 'God be with you, my children. God will guide you safely home.'

We moved away, gradually, while Josef waved to us with a white rag, until we could no longer see the splash of white in the crowded road which wound through pensive coppices of misted green and bulging slopes covered with young woodland.

From time to time we would stop and talk with others among the hundreds of refugees. Some were in even worse circumstances than ourselves; but even in that degree of extreme poverty and suffering there were those who remained quite jovial about their own fate.

We walked at a slow pace until our feet could carry us no further and we were forced to rest by the roadside. While we were sleeping someone stole Josef's bundle with all our food. Nevertheless, we saw one group of refugees nearby absorbed in distributing the daily bread rations – one piece per person, about the size of a biscuit. We emerged from behind the crowd and got a few crumbs enough to keep us going.

After a cordial conversation, Tonia and I were on our way yet again. The war may well have ended for those who had been undisturbed by the savage Nazis, but for us it seemed there was no end.

*

Convoys of army trucks filled with soldiers advanced along the rolling mountains towards the sun-drenched countryside around Lienz. Often, they would honk their horns to clear the road as they approached each bend. At times we had to jump off the road like rabbits: we were only too happy to get out of their way as long as we were left alone. The Allied soldiers were still unfamiliar to us and we remained wary of them as the Nazi propaganda was still ringing in our ears. Just before we left Vienna the Germans had repeatedly broadcast their warnings over the radio: the Americans and the British will rape, loot, and kill.

But we need not have worried. Once or twice, the soldiers jumped off their trucks and ran along by the roadside: they threw us a loaf of white bread and a little square of chocolate, from their personal rations. To this day I often bless them for that generosity: they will never know how much it was appreciated by those two humble refugees.

*

The breeze fell in the afternoon; we felt hot and thirsty. For some time now Tonia's words had been spirited away due to the weakness of her voice. We were gradually turning the longest bend ever when I heard a dog howl somewhere in the distance. Then . . . I experienced an immediate thrill of expectation: like a miracle, right down in the valley was the joyous sight of a church tower, vague in colour, but its top glistening in the sunshine. Traditional-style houses were clustered together, undisturbed by war: pretty and colourful, the little town of Lienz lay where the River Drau meandered quietly along the Drau valley.

We drew closer. The branches of a willow tree dipped gently in and out of the clear water; on the green banks of the river two white cows were tugging at the long grass and a young foal rubbed its hind against an old tree-trunk.

We soon were able to take a closer look at the people of Lienz: they wore extremely resentful expressions on their faces and were far from eager to help us when we had asked for directions to the railway station. We were not really surprised that the Austrians were so curt to us, as the overcrowded streets of their town were bursting with refugees, British soldiers and men of foreign nationality, yet dressed in German Wehrmacht uniforms, who lined the narrow square by the post office building in their thousands.

Outside the grey post office there lay a gigantic pile of ammunition, crudely abandoned and perishing under the sky. Tonia and I were resting in the church grounds on the opposite side of the square when we saw in the midst of the ragged refugees a man, conspicuously dressed in German uniform with Cossack headgear, riding a beautiful black horse through the iron gate. This was incomprehensible to us: we had no idea who those people were, or indeed, why they were in Lienz.

Vast groups of energetic men were parading in and out of the building, collecting their portion of delicious-smelling goulash – provided exclusively for the German-uniformed people. When the lovely smell reached my nostrils I went across and also joined the queue. One sympathetic officer tried to explain that the food was issued only to the military personnel, but, I told him that *my* Russian stomach was just as hungry as *his*! He ended up by carrying two metal bowls of goulash to where Tonia was resting! He was so engrossed with my impertinence that he had forgotten to get his own food and thus he stayed with us for hours.

Daniel Yakovlev was a noticeably tall and dark young Cossack from General Domanov's division, who had fought side by side with the Germans. Many of them were blackmailed by the Germans, he told us: if they had not fought the war with them, they would have been sent to Auschwitz or other Nazi concentration camps. They were faced with an impossible dilemma: if they had chosen not to fight they would have been shot in Block 11 at Auschwitz in the same manner as most of the Red Army who were captured by the Germans.

The Cossack officer's head slumped against his chest. Tears were visible in his blue eyes as he uttered, 'The Cossacks and those of us who are still in uniform, have unfinished quarrels with the Soviets. Our struggle against Communism had ended in great disappointment even before we had to surrender to our much-respected Western allies.' A torment of loss wrenched his mind.

At first, try as I might, I was unable to understand the full implications of his story. I understood even less the reasons why they could not return to their homes in Russia, where most of their relatives were left behind. I suppose that Tonia and I were still brimming with our good fortune in having managed to reach as far as Lienz. God willing, we might go further tomorrow. If we could do it, why could not they? I wondered also why on earth they were still wearing that frightful uniform?

Daniel, who had no family with him, tried to flirt a little with Tonia, and to persuade her to stay with the unit. But Tonia disliked the uniform so much that, in a flash, she spat on his Wehrmacht jacket, got up and walked away. Nothing could anchor us now in any foreign country.

We left the *Hauptplatz* and after we had walked for about fifteen minutes we came upon a huge encampment which seemed to stretch endlessly along the Drau valley. It was called Peggetz Camp and consisted of wooden barracks, long deserted by the Germans and now refilled with the sound of vibrating voices in many languages. We did not register at the main gate and walked in a forlorn mood along the grey dusty path, surveying each barrack as we passed it. I can remember the whole area being crowded with people to such a degree that I could not see the neatly cut grass underneath.

Throughout our stay in Lienz, we were treated the same as all those several thousand women, children and prisoners-of-war, who had been coerced by the Nazi propaganda. Some of the mothers had been forced to earn bread for their children behind the barbed wire, while their men were enticed into the Wehrmacht. A number of the younger women in the communal barrack displayed evasively disturbing looks of humiliation: they were reasonably well-fed, but were dressed in rags. The men were oppressed by the deep anguish of disillusion: they all wore very shabby and faded, but still recognisable, Wehrmacht uniforms.

It was somehow frightening to see the Drau Valley so overladen with its cavalcade of thousands of Cossacks and their horses of all different shapes and sizes. The horses grazed for miles over the wide green landscape. Clusters of carts littered the valley, their canvases blown by the wind, and their owners stood tensely by them in groups looking dazed and bewildered.

Ivan Petrovitch was one of these men. He was of a dumpy frame, with luminous black eyes, and sounded quite absurd as he told his corny story, leaning against an extended cart. The women listening to him, as they roasted potatoes on the huge bonfire, did not seem to find him very amusing!

Under the long wooden bridge over the River Drau there were

groups of people swimming in the nude while the more energetic youngsters played with a ball, and several older women, their children by their side, were mending their badly worn out clothing. We, too, took off our coats and footwear (at least what was left of it) and went for a swim, staying close to the river bank.

We lay down on the grass to let our clothes dry in the sun before going back to the barracks. But we were still wet when we eventually walked up the narrow little path looking for a vacant corner in which we could stay. We had decided to make the camp our base at least until we found some kind of work and enough money to provide our fares to Russia.

It was a grey-bearded Orthodox priest who showed us which barrack had a spare space: he then made a sign of the cross over our faces and said, comfortingly, 'You look as though you have travelled rough, my children. Where are you from?'

Tonia just glanced at him sharply, but he did not ask any more questions, merely adding, 'If you have difficulty in finding a place in the barrack you can share with us that green tent by the river.'

'We won't be needing a tent, as we'll be going home to Russia very soon,' replied Tonia, quickly.

He stared unbelievingly and shook his head. A fine line from his high cheek bone climbed up towards his transparent blue eyes and his heavy eyelids slowly opened and closed as he scanned our care-worn, bedraggled appearance. 'I hope, my children, that you will not be disappointed with your foolish plans'. With another sign of the cross he turned and walked off in the opposite direction.

Why should we be disappointed with our plans, I thought? After all, we are non-political animals and only sixteen: all we want is to be reunited with our loved ones.

Just before we reached the first barrack Tonia became even more apprehensive than she had been previously and in two minds whether to remain even for a while in Peggetz. It was the sight of a large number of men in Wehrmacht uniforms parading in the camp's square which troubled her. It brought suddenly to the surface, for both of us, memories of the Germans' ferocity which still hovered in our minds. My mind always became muddled whenever I tried to shut out the image of those black SS uniforms and the villains inside them and I would search instead for my happiest memories: those of my schooldays and my chestnut horse. Perhaps Mishka would be waiting for me on my return, by the apple tree where I always used to tie her; we could bounce away to the steppes and then to the forest, galloping for many kilometres towards the horizon.

*

The low wooden building of the barrack smelled of dampness and stale tobacco. It was divided into several sections, some of which were separated by only a torn grey blanket. I tapped my feet noisily on the wooden floor by a second entrance and a woman of medium height and with an ailing face, came through and stood in front of me. Cradled in her arms was a crying child, who was six years old, but very tiny for his age. Tolya's Mama had been killed in Italy only a few months previously: his Papa, who served in a Cossack division, had been lost in action during the fierce battle for Tolmezzo. Little Tolya was all his grandmother had left to remind her of her late daughter's marriage. A round iron stove was prominently positioned in the middle of the barrack. The floor it stood on was so warped that you could almost lose your foot in between the floorboards. Dasha Alexandrovna put Tolya down and brushed her hands on her brown dress. She turned abruptly, before examining herself critically in the faded old mirror which hung behind her: her dress bulged around her waist-line and hung loosely in folds almost down to her ankles.

We learned that she had been living in exile since the Russian Revolution when her family were forced to flee to Yugoslavia. I could see that the poor woman had experienced her share of agony and was nearly out of her mind: all she could do now was pray deliriously to God for guidance.

The barrack was like a railway station during the brief time that we stood there; people came and went, asking us where we were from, always hoping to find someone from their own home. For a while I forgot my own hunger and poverty as I listened intently to their many personal tragedies, all inflicted by the Nazis in one way or another. I knew only too well that their unbelievable statements were true.

Some of the fierce-looking soldiers engaged in a spirited debate. One of them outlined his own justification of his plight: he had reached despair a long time ago through witnessing the gauntlet of Communism strangle the life of his Russian people and thus had tried to prove to himself mathematically that he should not run from the battle and should fight side by side with the Germans.

114

'I have fought and killed in my own town – and it was *real* fighting. Well,' he said, 'I had to . . .'.

The rest of the men muttered and cursed the Germans, frowning with animated displeasure.

The soldiers appeared drained and lethargic: it may have been because there was no one left to issue orders to these normally disciplined men. And – unknown to me at the time – their ears were already being filled with ominous rumours about their fate.

We were to learn of other reasons underlying the atmosphere of disquiet: the barracks had already generated strange and unspeakable hatreds between Caucasians, Poles, Greeks, Turks and even Jews. In addition, SS men were said to be masquerading as refugees, the Germans as Austrians, the Austrians as Dutch, and some women were even dressed in men's uniforms! *All* were denouncing the enemy. Men ran here and there, seeking roads of escape. And there was no Nazi to be found.

Dasha Alexandrovna put her work-stained hand on my shoulder and pushed back a loose strand of hair off my eyebrows. She looked at me with affection and told me sadly, 'Your lovely green eyes do so much resemble those of my late daughter Nadina when she was your age.'

My throat seemed full of little knots; I could not get the right word out. Her right hand gently brushed my pale bony cheeks before she disappeared into her cubicle and brought back several articles of clothing which had belonged to Nadina.

That night Tonia and I slept on a spotlessly clean bunk against a wall. Our living space was separated from the rest by a grey blanket which Dasha Alexandrovna provided and contained a white enamel basin and a pail of water, resting on an empty wooden box. I was ever so thankful for the lady's kindness and no sooner had I stretched my tired body on the bunk than I fell asleep.

I was wakened the following morning by the daylight flooding in through the tiny window and a most piercing whistle let loose by the little boy. I sat up and wondered where I was! Tonia was still fast asleep on the upper bunk: her thin face looked weary and lifeless.

I gasped when I noticed the beautiful pale green dress and brown laced shoes which Dasha Alexandrovna had set out for me to wear – they were fit for a princess, I thought. Tonia managed to fit her taller body into a dark blue gusseted *sarafan*, made of a coarser cloth than mine. The clothes were clean, fresh and most elegantly

115

styled by war standards. My heart leaped with sheer excitement and gratitude. I was ready to face another new phase in my young life.

A faint streak of hope entered my mind: the camp was, after all, in the most capable and humane hands of the British, controlled by the 8th Battalion Argyll and Sutherland Highlanders. I doubted if one could have found a more capable liaison officer than Major Davies, whom we called 'Rusty' for short. The British soldiers were of extremely smart appearance and walked in great numbers around the Drau valley, always so friendly and jovial. The younger children often followed the soldiers around and were given sweets by them. Even the two shaggy dogs wagged their tails in a playful manner, and yelped from excitement when the British soldiers patted and fed them.

Tolya was a demanding and boisterous blue-eyed boy, but loveable and totally spoiled by everyone, especially by the British soldiers who frequently lavished him with sweets and chocolates from their own issue.

I have a fleeting recollection of Tolya and I going to the furthest away hut (which was used as a kitchen): we were given a packet of cream crackers and some marmalade. At lunchtime, the potato soup had that same appetising aroma which I had smelled at home. There was also the bonus of two slices of white bread. When we had put it all on the makeshift table we felt like millionaires! Our conversation lapsed discreetly into silence, as though we were staging a dumb show: we could not find enough good words to praise the kind-hearted British personnel.

Days passed by. I felt ever so much better than before, as I basked contentedly in the warmth of the British protection. A veritable crowd of orphans had also found shelter under their care: there were those whose families had been killed at some point during the war and a host of others whose parents had died in the Nazi concentration camps. For all of us, whatever our circumstances, the British became an indispensable part of our lives. Life ran normally once more.

CHAPTER SIX

YALTA VICTIM

During our prayers, Tonia and I often went down on our knees to demonstrate our most grateful thanks to God. But even during those prayers, my heart ached for Mama and the urgent wish nagged deep inside me, so much so that I walked to Lienz and begged for work. I was willing to do any kind of work – in the kitchens or in the fields – but there was none. The Austrians, and understandably so, took preference over anybody else. I cried a little. Thoughts thronged in my head, but there was no one to share them with as I walked back towards the now familiar square in Lienz.

Glancing over the foliage in the distance, I could just see two pairs of legs sticking out, rigid and straight. Tonia and Daniel were caught in a hurried embrace. Occasionally, the strikingly handsome Daniel turned and stirred his body into brilliant exertions.

The panic grew in my mind at the thought that Tonia might stay with Daniel and I would have to find my way home on my own. There were more than twenty thousand Cossacks at the settlement: surely there would be someone going my way. If only I could find that certain somebody I would be quite happy. I could have wept in my longings.

I felt the separation as greatly as the day when I was first taken away. I had a scorching thirst: my body was calling for food and my feet were like two big sores. My heart groaned a little as I staggered on to the camp.

*

Easter was a day of hope and glory, despite the world of difference between sisters and brothers. The service was held in the fields. The bearded Orthodox priests in their colourful robes bellowed their vibrating voices along the Drau valley: 'Christ is Risen!' Thousands of hearts cried out in reply, 'Christ is Risen!' confessing their sins. I saw one Cossack whose knees buckled listlessly as he shouted out his secret torments.

The make-shift altar was at its most beautiful, decorated with garlands of delightful wild flowers which we had gathered and strewn in front of it earlier that morning. The priests had been captivated as

119

they chatted and laughed light-heartedly, succumbing to the charm of young children. As 'Christ is Risen!' echoed, we embraced and kissed each other in every corner of the meadows in the valley. The service passed in high spirits.

That evening the balalaikas and harmonicas played intoxicating strains of gypsy polkas, which stirred the blood of the young as well as the grey-headed: they snapped their fingers, beating time with their feet. Daniel and Tonia danced the mazurka as though there would be no tomorrow! I was wrapped in admiration to see them so happy together. But Tonia's fatigue soon became severe and, panting heavily, she abandoned the floor and contented herself with watching the more energetic crowd floating in the forefront. Some of the men had pinned our wild flowers to their breast pockets: the women wore them in their hair – they all looked very colourful.

We had nothing else to offer – and would gather and present our wild flowers when we wished to express our gratitude. On some occasions we showered passing cars full of British soldiers with wild flowers. In turn, they waved to us, blowing kisses with cordial assurance of their goodwill.

The kind of freedom which existed in the camp was bliss for the majority of refugees, who had earlier been oppressed by the Nazi tyranny. Consequently we looked upon the British as our saviours – suffused with warmth and understanding. But there was one thing that I could not understand: the fighting Cossacks still had their wives and families with them. Some of the aged men should have been in their rocking chairs playing with their grandchildren at their time of life and not in this scene of slow strangulation. I was told that they all maintained a singleness of purpose, fanaticism even, in their violent resentment against Communism, and that they were willing to die for this cause. I personally did not pay much attention to the politics in the camp and lived my short spell there in a child-like simplicity.

Whenever there was a heated argument in the barrack, as often happened, Tonia and I would duly take Tolya for a walk. One evening, towards the end of May, a ferocious debate woke me up in the early hours of the morning. The priest had come to tell the barrack about certain betrayal and the quarrel which followed nearly ended up in blows. Many harsh words were spoken, including some references related to the 'Forcible Repatriation' ... I had found myself a victim of the secret Yalta Agreement which took place between Stalin, Churchill and Roosevelt in February 1945, and which is still furiously defended even today: tales of hesitation and uncertainty on the part of those in high places remain obscured so that the real facts will never be known. But in plain words Stalin demanded the return of all Soviet citizens by force if necessary and irrespective of their wishes.

Tonia and I were not really concerned about the rumours of the forthcoming repatriation because we *wished* to return to our homeland. At the same time, I felt contemptuous pity for Dasha Alexandrovna and her grandchild Tolya, when she expressed her fear of being punished by the Soviets, especially when she herself had no desire to go anywhere.

I linked my arm around Alexandrovna's and asked her if she had a scrap of paper on which I could write a note home. However, when I made enquiries later at the post office in Lienz, I was upset to hear that there was no post to or from the Soviet Union. I felt so miserable and unhappy and envied the Austrians who seemed able to live a normal life. I passed the well-stocked gardens, filled with shrubs and flowers, belonging to a two-storey house. The walls were plastered with climbing wild vines, their small branches caressing the window sills with their tendrils; even that pretty picture failed to raise my spirits.

It was to the Austrian people that I looked for some fragment of compassion: sadly, they were the same as the Germans. They were fully prepared to let the refugees from our camp work on their farms in return for a plate of soup, but no more.

That day I was only aware of the road on which I walked back to Peggetz, and nothing else: my mind was too preoccupied with the obstacles which crossed my path each time I tried to make contact with my home. Each of my wishes had been like a magnificent old ruin with its massive rust-eaten columns crumbling and corroding to stare in sorrow upon the world.

I came to my senses at the sight of an unusually large crowd of British soldiers in the camp. Any other time there would have been many children tugging at the soldiers' uniforms, and I wondered why not now. I felt, too, rather a strange pulse inside me.

I was not surprised that the whole camp was in mourning when I learned that, on Major Arbuthnott's orders, the British soldiers had taken away hundreds of the best Cossack horses. Afterwards, the camp's opinion of the British was at its lowest. The world has condemned the Nazi barbarians when *they* stole and confiscated other people's property. Was Major Arbuthnott's action any different?

It was such a great transformation from the day before, when

General Andrei Shkuro had visited the camp. We had all lined the path: men, women and children laughing and shouting, 'Hurrah! Hurrah!' at the cheery father-like figure as he waved to us in triumph.

*

Towards the end of May the rumours about the Forcible Repatriation were more positive and spread throughout the camp like wildfire. One evening, the priest again stormed into our hut. He looked around searchingly as everyone gathered to listen to what he had to say: only to hear a firm confirmation of the rumours. Our energy drained away as we listened to his words. We clung closely to our newly formed little family unit: Alexandrovna put her hand around Tonia, while Tolya was fast asleep with his head over my shoulder.

The priest strode suddenly towards the door, his strong features black with rage. 'Come on my people,' he bellowed, 'we must pray. Only prayers will save us from the iron claws of Communism.'

That night we were asked to help prepare the simple decoration for the altar. We all obliged most willingly.

*

It was 28 May 1945, and thousands of solemn faces watched all the Cossack officers being loaded on to the British trucks for a pre-arranged conference with Field Marshal Alexander, which was to take place in Spittal, only about an hour's drive from Lienz. By that time the rumours had reached a peak — particularly about the dubious 'conference' — and for this very reason the Cossack officers scrambled into the British trucks with their minds gyrating like anguished savages. It was like wartime all over again: people were saying goodbye to each other; wild-eyed officers' wives were weeping, amazed at the sudden and furious disturbance; their screaming children held on to their fathers' jackets.

The wife of one of the officers, in an advanced stage of pregnancy, asked in despair if she could go with her husband. When this was denied she held on to the moving truck as though she already knew that she would never see him again, until her tired body crumpled limply in the dust. Another woman naïvely had begged the interpreter to ask the British driver when their husbands would return.

'We'll be back in the afternoon, or early in the evening if there is no delay,' the driver replied, without committing himself.

As the trucks proceeded on their way passing swiftly by the huge crowd, one of the Cossacks called out, joyfully, 'We'll be back for dinner.'

After the officers had gone, the atmosphere in the camp was like that immediately after a statesman's funeral: clusters of people were discussing at length whether or not the British had invented the conference. But it was far too late: they had all gone, enticed, like poor little lambs to the slaughter. The Cossack officers did not return that evening – and my recollection of that evil event remains deeply imprinted in my mind, even today.

When the transport returned empty without the Cossacks, the very air struck terror in Peggetz. A combination of tempers and prayers raged through the night. Worse still, in the gaping darkness, one of the officers who had somehow managed to escape crawled back into the camp. Lifeless and badly bleeding about the chest, pulsating saliva running from the corners of his mouth, he delivered his gigantic curses to the faces around him.

'The British have lied and betrayed us,' he sobbed. His thin body vibrated from weakness, but he carried on talking: 'The Soviets snarled at our men like wild wolves and then they shot them in the woods. We were handed over to . . .' He suddenly lurched forward and lapsed into silence.

After this incident all hell was let loose in the barracks: cries of pain and agony about the British soldiers handing over the very first bunch of Cossack officers carried far and wide. I became engulfed in a delirium of despair and death: I, too, was now afraid of that kind of punishment.

But what had *I* done wrong, to justify being killed by my own people, in my own homeland because of which I had put up such an intense struggle to survive? All my hopes of seeing Mama and my relatives fled. What an awful realisation for a girl of sixteen to face.

Small patches of morning mist floated before my vision as I brushed the tears from my face, forcing out the single comforting thought that there must have been some misunderstanding: the British soldiers have kind hearts – surely they would not let us all be shot by the Soviets? Never before had my teeth chattered as nervously as they did that day, not even when I had been caught under a shower of bombs.

At last, Major Davies made the official announcement. He told us that it was true that the Cossack officers had been handed over to the Soviets. I did not want to believe it. He wore a deeply disturbed expression, making it impossible for anyone to believe his reassurance that the Cossacks would be treated benevolently by the Soviets. Pausing for a moment, Major Davies had to face a mass of weeping people breathlessly shouting out their protest.

No one could sleep that night. We gathered every available scrap of black material, made black flags and placed them on every barrack and tent and also along the main road between Lienz and Oberdrauburg.

A hunger strike was declared and the food which was brought by the British into the camp was left untouched. As the huge piles accumulated we put a pole through the middle supporting yet another black flag. There were many placards erected too, which declared in faulty English: 'Better death here than our sending into the USSR!'

Dasha Alexandrovna, who was already in mourning for her loved ones, had her black dress made into flags. We held a religious service, throughout which the younger members of the congregation held black flags in the air waving to the British soldiers as they went up and down through the camp. The sight filled me with wonder.

Some Cossacks were openly weeping as they stood by their faithful friends − their horses. For a long time they had shared together their hardships and happiness throughout the war and during the arduous journey from Russia. Mr Komarovski, who lived in our hut, could not bear to part with his much-loved black horse: he led him over the bridge and into the woodland, and after stroking the animal's head tenderly, he took out his hidden revolver and shot it through the head. The lustre faded from his eyes, expressing his profound dejection. Tonia and I were shocked as we watched him carry out the execution.

*

Unknown to us at the time the full implications of the Yalta Agreement were already being enforced throughout Germany, Austria, Italy and Britain. Here, nearer our camp, a grim darkness was aimed directly over Oberdrauburg, which was bedevilled with ghastly forms of the Forcible Repatriation. Unnumbered thousands were loaded into trains: men, women and children, to be sent to Judenburgh where the Soviets were allowed to conduct the shootings in an old steel mill.

We too, began to feel the effects of repatriation. From the smoke-infested Drau valley came a swarm of running Cossacks, swinging their black flags from all angles − like unbalanced urchins.

The time drew closer. Major Davies returned to the camp and

announced the unpleasant news that the repatriation would take place tomorrow, on 1 June 1945. A burning roar filled my ears; tears were streaming down my cheeks. I put my hands over my ears saying, 'Oh no, I don't want to hear it.'

Tolya was by my side and kept tugging at my skirt and repeating, 'Don't cry, don't cry'. He then asked his grandmama, 'Why are you crying?' Like any nervous child watching other people crying, Tolya started to scream until his screams turned into wheezing asthma. Other children had joined Tolya's screams and their faces were pitiful in their plight.

Major Davies was as sympathetic as he could be and tried exceedingly hard to reassure the future enforced repatriates of their safety once they reached their destination. But his honest expression and the blood rushing to his face betrayed him. We knew that he was not telling the true facts of the matter. After the announcement, the crowd replied with curses and shouted to the Major to be damned. I was still unable to visualise the reality that was to follow.

That night, the dark blue sky was mottled with grey clouds. We looked up to heaven and prayed hard for our salvation. The reassuring words of Major Davies echoed in my ears but the adverse thoughts so overpowered them that my body became drenched in cold sweat. The camp and tents were in an uproar of sleepless turmoil; some people had gathered their small possessions together and were walking away across the narrow wooden bridge which led into the mountains. Dim lights flickered all over the valley and tongues of fire leapt from the mouths of those whose lives were in an immediate danger – only hours away.

One Cossack who waded across the fast-flowing river questioned another with distaste: 'Why are the British siding with the Soviets?'

'Pahh . . .' exclaimed a third, sucking his pipe deeply into his large chest. 'Is this the way of British freedom and justice?' He kept his eyes watchfully upon the dark clouds. 'First we were tricked by the British into exchanging our old arms for the new ones – when there was nothing the matter with our old arms – and now we are left with no arms, not even a weapon left with which to commit suicide.' It was indeed true that the British had removed all the Cossacks' weapons, but many of them had hidden revolvers and rifles among their personal belongings.

Another man, his eyes burning with hate and still wearing his German uniform, was distributing his much-treasured possessions to the Austrians or whoever else wished to take them. He would not need them where he was going, in the Soviet Union. Other small groups of people had their own objections to this evil threat: they all groaned, 'Oh Lord...' on their knees, praying for mercy. But the kind of mercy *they* were looking for blew only cold winds over the camp.

The Cossacks themselves were considered traitors for their complicity with the Germans, but what about the women and the children? There were many people who had come from different concentration camps, like Tonia and I who were far too young to do any harm even to an animal – least of all a country! Indeed, what right had the British, or any other nation for that matter, to attack unarmed Cossacks, refugees, some only babies, so eagerly and so savagely?

The night passed more quickly than usual. By the early morning an improvised platform in the camp square had been erected. The makeshift altar was surrounded by beautiful icons, colourful banners and large wooden crosses. The Orthodox priests were dressed in their vestments, with chains and crosses on their chests; they also held crosses and icons in their hands. On three sides of the square a frail fence had been erected, leaving one side open for escape, but the children disregarded the open space and made equal use of all sides. By six thirty in the morning the mournful crowd had sprung from all corners of the camp and the valley and in a short time the square was filled with three to four thousand quivering people.

*

The scent of peaceful willows was in our nostrils as Tonia and I called at the camp's hospital barrack for our friend Sonia Pavlova before joining Dasha Alexandrovna on the square. Sonia was still busy tending to a few minor casualties. She bandaged the injured hand of her last patient as she recalled incidents from her happy childhood in her native Odessa and her escape from Dachau concentration camp. Indeed, she remembered all her fortunes of yesterday.

Skinny as a lath and as sharp as a needle, her simple words touched me deeply as she spoke of her fears of being returned to the Soviets by force. She said with a soft voice, 'I smell evil – the whole mess is going to explode in our faces and the politicians might utilise it for their own ends.' It did not mean much to me then, but it has cast a shadow on later history.

Sonia did not really wish to go to the square but thought it was better to be together with the rest of the people. So the three of us joined the huge mass in their deep prayers. The Russian liturgy emerged from the altar: the crosses were held in nervous hands as they swayed above the heads and the black flags were flapping in the gentle June breeze. The morning dew filled the Drau with transparent silver, and smouldering fires were scattered about the grassy banks. Everything was entirely and peacefully quiet: only the insects were making their rhythmical noises.

The congregation bore a sickly colour in their eyes and their faces. Tonia and I moved towards the altar. Tonia held my hand firmly while Dasha Alexandrovna, with Tolya perched on her shoulders, followed right behind us. There were no stars in the lovely blue sky, yet during the Lord's Prayer a flurry of shining bright light, like rain, descended upon the praying crowd. I felt a wierd sensation and gave a loud cry of exasperation. Was that the Holy Spirit upraising the ghosts of shame? It has made me wonder ever since.

The priest cleared his throat. His bearded face was expressionless, but his most powerful voice echoed memorably over the whole square. Tears were streaming down his dark beard; his hands were outstretched in a shape of a cross towards the sky. 'God give me the answer for my people,' he sang.

Women and children were positioned in the middle of the square, while the men and young boys had formed a protective cordon around us. No one had any intention of co-operating with the British nor did we intend to move away from the square until the matter had been resolved in an amiable manner. We still hoped for an answer to the camp's petition for clemency which had been sent to King George, the International Red Cross, King Peter of Yugoslavia and Field Marshal Alexander.

The British soldiers were smartly dressed – men to be proud of – bright and shining in their uniforms, as though they were ready for the King's inspection and most certainly not for killing anyone. But the final moment came, and Major Davies commanded the soldiers to fix bayonets.

'It is time for loading,' he said and waited, looking horrified as he listened for our reaction. At his words, the crowd tightened resolutely and our voices rose as we sang, *Svataya Maria (Holy Mary)*. We were very afraid but did not stop singing.

I had forgotten my own hunger, but wondered what those well-fed soldiers had eaten that morning to make them be in such a hurry to send us on the death-road to the Soviets. Surely they could find some excuse to delay this outcome. Even up until that time I had not believed that the British – the kind-hearted soldiers – would harm innocent people.

But I was wrong. During the Lord's Prayer, I watched the soldiers' bayonets glisten in the sun as they advanced on the mass. At the first tug by the soldiers the earth shook violently underneath us, like a volcano: our bodies were crushed together so closely that a needle could not have passed in between them. Another tug... and the Lord's Prayer was drowned in screams as the soldiers pitched forward insanely, moblike and barbaric, with an enthusiasm well beyond the bounds of control. The mass of humans huddled together, delirious with despair, like animals hypnotised by the sight and smell of blood. We were crouching with our arms interlocked.

There was a pause for a moment, then the soldiers answered in the same way they would have gone into battle. At first they attacked us with their rifle butts and big sticks while trying to pull away a group of people from the outermost perimeter of the circle. At that point, a fight broke out as women from inside the circle tried to help their men to resist the soldiers. The soldiers then fired shots. The song of bullets and shells snarled directly over the crowd: some on the outside fell in grotesque agonies from their injuries, others were stunned by sheer fright.

I was in the centre of the circle and only just managed to hear Tonia, who by then was some distance behind me: she was screaming and waving her hand. 'Come on!' she roared, 'We'll all be killed if we stay here.'

I lost sight of her hand when I was suddenly hoisted up above the crowd like a football. I could feel the humid flesh and the heads underneath my feet, but could do nothing except watch the hysterical battle in full view below me. There were many howls and decisive blows as the soldiers dragged away first the men, then the women, children and tiny babies, loading them into the waiting army trucks.

The bayonets were now in full use; the rifle butts were swinging amongst the helpless crowd. In their swift and deadly rushes to attack the men the British soldiers yelled like lunatics. Just two yards away from the circle one soldier was bending over a man who was lying flat on the ground with blood spurting from his head. The blood soiled the soldier's face, but another soldier came quickly to help him and together they lifted the unconscious man and threw him into the truck.

On the south side of the square a group of Cossacks wrestled with the soldiers, leaping like hounds. Underneath their feet lay a woman in the last month of pregnancy. She lay on her back in a most uninhibited fashion, her hands flung above her head and her legs parted — unable to protect the small life inside her. Today, the baby boy crushed in his mother's abdomen is a living reminder of that evil event. He was born spastic and totally unable to comprehend the injustice he was subjected to in the warmth of his mother's womb. In 1975, when I made my first pilgrimage to Lienz, that very child had grown into a tall young man: he was living in the suburbs of Lienz — only a short distance from that scene of death.

*

The sun shed its light over the fighting men, but light alone does not convey the wisdom of understanding this form of persecution. I really thought by now that the soldiers' minds must have blacked out. Why had they been so kind in the first instance only to behave so badly and turn against us so cruelly? Indeed, I realised even then that they must have been compelled by political powers beyond their control to act as they did, astonishing as it was. They were infused with such madness that it was almost unnatural. To me, it was even more unnatural to see the soldiers crying even as they proceeded with their actions.

No amount of crying or begging from the kneeling mother could stop the soldier pulling her little girl from her arms and flinging her into the truck. Another freckle-faced, red-headed soldier slowly lifted his rifle and grabbed the priest by his dark robes. Tears were streaming from his undefinably coloured eyes as he pursued his 'enemy', but the priest pushed him away with a large wooden cross. The priest then deposited himself firmly on the platform before yet another attack plunged deeper into the circle and the altar collapsed with its icons and decorations showering the crowd. In the resulting chaos a pyramid of screaming humans clambered over each other, frantically trying to free themselves and get away from the soldiers' hands. More blood and destruction.

But the power of the British seemed stronger than ours as they illustrated the extent of their capabilities — carrying out their orders with a cool professional skill. They filled the waiting trucks with people despite the injuries and protests. The British officer who was in command growled angrily at the soldiers: his reasons became obvious a moment later.

They swung their weapons vigorously at us from all angles and pulled the reluctant victims by their limbs. I really thought that I had had it.

At that moment, I was lifted once more by the mob and thrown like an eggshell against the window of a hut. Through the split glass, the upper part of me fell inside the hut: but my legs were trapped on the other side and my knees impaled on the jagged glass. I was pinned tightly on both sides. At first the pain was severe, but then I could no longer feel anything from the waist down. People were swarming over me. It seemed hours until Tonia, too, was pushed to the hut; she managed somehow to throw my legs inside. But it was useless – I could not move an inch. The wooden floor of the hut was strewn with glass, broken bottles, plates, and cutlery. This part of the hut must have been someone's treasured home only a few hours before this sudden upheaval.

Tonia's protection over my body did not last long as people continued to pour through the window like a mountain stream, trampling over us as though we were not there. I could hear Tonia's commanding voice saying, 'Get up, get up, you can walk', while she frantically pulled and tugged me by my arms half across the floor. In one swift movement I got up, stumbled and fell again, but with Tonia supporting me we hastened towards the bridge over the River Drau.

I could hear the inhuman whistling in the air and people were falling with moans and shrieks. My own legs were torn to ribbons: chunks of flesh were missing and the loss of blood made me lag behind, frequently falling in the tall grass. We stopped for a moment by the river, and tore a piece of dress to try and bandage my wounds. It was pointless: the rags quickly became saturated in blood and slipped off my legs.

My senses were so deadened by weakness that, at times, even Tonia's voice sounded distant. The whole valley was shimmering in the heat and the grass was rippling gently in the breeze. It would have been a day in which to celebrate the joy of being alive if it was not for the crude scene before our eyes. Valiant fugitives were darting like rabbits in all directions. Their faces revealed an agony of fear and rage as they tried to flee the showers of bullets. The poor Cossacks' horses were trampling all over the valley – lost without their owners.

The guns from the rear raged right over to the mountains across the Drau. The injured were lying all over the vast valley, many of them still conscious but stunned – their spirits worn by distress. Tonia and I stumbled over a boy of my own age, whose mangled body was beyond help: he sprawled like an animal after being thrashed, his face covered with a mixture of earth and blood. Bravely, he raised his head as though he knew it was for the last time and when the last breath had left him ... his sightless eyes continued to stare at the deserted sky.

The British soldiers carried on sullenly with their task: an air of despair coloured their attitude as they grabbed as many unwilling fugitives as they could and jostled them towards the crammed trucks. I saw the heart-rending scene of one soldier gesticulating with a Cossack while another was chasing a young boy on horseback who galloped and waved his hands with goodwill.

Shooting, and more shooting, echoed in our ears as Tonia and I approached the path to the wooden bridge. We could see fresh patches of blood where people had been before us. For this was the path which would eventually lead us across the River Drau and deep into the Alps. When eventually we reached the bridge we found a hysterical crowd of women with their children and babies. They cried out savagely before plunging into the River Drau like flies. Mrs Ignatova was one of them, a middle-aged woman whose long hair was wondrously tousled over her forehead. Her two children had already hit the black-veined water when she crossed herself three times and jumped after them; in seconds even her head had vanished under the icy waves. Ironically, the hot sun had triggered off a sudden thaw in the mountains which had caused the river to swell with freezing water, offering the victims little or no chance of survival.

We searched vainly for Tolya and Alexandrovna, but to our horror Alexandrovna was already shoulder deep in water. Her mouth was wide open and she was gazing at Tolya's little blue jacket which was flapping in the water before her eyes. But there was no sign of Tolya. On the other side of the bridge a soldier was desperately trying to pull somebody out of the deep water. In full uniform he was talking to him as he studied the stiffening condition of his body. Dasha Alexandrovna had noticed the soldiers. She seemed to be experiencing a moment's torment and she waved to us before the fast current swept her along the Drau. We never saw her or Tolya again.

The soldiers were lurking far too close for comfort on the banks of the river and we ran across the bridge towards the shadows of the mountains. We heard persistent shouts rise from the water like those of ghosts crying in sharp agony. The wooden bridge swayed, creaked and groaned with the heavy feet thundering over it. There were those whose minds were defeated by a vision of death, who dropped off the side with a twisting movement into the grey water.

Tonia and I reached the other side safely, but the suicide voices remained stubbornly in my ears, together with the wild emotional screams for mercy. The lovely June summer's day had turned into a vision of infinite ugliness.

The sun was stabbing the mountainside with its fiery arrows. One Cossack ahead of us was swaying as he ran, the sweat trickling down his neck and face. His right hand was bleeding, but he kept going, pulling the two elderly women behind him towards the Alps and deep into the dark woodland. I had turned anxiously to see if the soldiers were coming after us, when I stumbled on a rock and fell flat on my face. With the added peril of a bleeding nose on top of the lack of feeling in my legs I just crawled under a huge clump of undergrowth and let fate take over.

I could not have walked even an inch further; the shadows of the trees danced crazily on the ground before my eyes. I could smell the sweet scent of pines, but could not get up even although I heard the nearby sound of raging bullets. Every bush was moving with fugitives seeking some respite, if only for a few hours before they too were caught and driven away in the cattle trucks which had been brought to the camp. I urged Tonia to leave me and go deeper into the Alps. Breaking the silence, she muttered, 'Ah, am I to leave you to the flies and mosquitos?' She pressed her hands to her temples and stretched her long legs under the undergrowth and said, 'We are safe here.'

We thought that we *were* safe and could stay quietly in the woods without being noticed, even though we were in full view of a white-painted farmhouse which belonged to an Austrian farmer. To the north of the farmhouse there were various inspiring green glades and pine woods, but no noticeable paths leading towards them. Even if there were, they would have been hidden by the thick layers of dead leaves. At that point, however, it was useless looking for a path which could lead us to the Alps, as the soldiers would have picked us up in no time: so we stayed put.

The afternoon heat brought swarms of large flies as well as many other unidentifiable hungry insects which sprang from the tree trunk, attracted by the sweet smell of blood on my legs. When Tonia pulled the undergrowth apart, the gap revealed a chaotic jumble of escapees. The faded colour of their faces shone courageously through the forest darkness.

I prayed aloud for help to get us further away from the farmhouse, but my words were lost in a roar of thunder from the soldiers' rifles. I could not stand it any longer and was trying painfully to move out into the open when I heard a startled cackle from the hens. I knew then that our safety was dangerously threatened. Tonia was engrossed in contemplation, and her lower lip quivered as she whispered, 'Here they come.'

Armed soldiers were carefully searching the farm for their victims, but in the end, they turned and continued their search in the opposite direction from where we were hiding. We could do nothing to solve our predicament, only trust that the Austrian farmer would have some compassion towards the strugglers for freedom hidden in the nearby woods. A young woman with a black shawl covering her shoulders was speeding forward and cooing to her little baby. Her song melted in the calm air as she bravely strode through the undulating grass and over the twigs. A large rabbit scurried between her thin legs and bounded off over the underwood.

'A bad omen,' I thought. But then, there were a lot of such superstitions in Russia, considered by many to be old wives' tales. At least that despairing woman had known the joy and fulfilment of motherhood – the kind of joy that the Nazis made sure that I will never know.

With a sudden impulse, I stood up, approached her and touched the baby's tiny hand in silence. And in silence the woman placed the baby deeper into my arms. After a few seconds they were on their way deep into the Alps.

Many years later – as time went by – my heart kept weeping for a baby, but my earliest unbearable fears were confirmed by a highly competent gynaecologist. That is why when people say, 'Let sleeping dogs lie', I feel hurt and the venomous brutalities of the SS revive in my mind along with the harrowing sadness that I will never have a child. And in the end, when I feel, as I often do, that the solid earth gives way underfoot and the world crumbles around my ears, I can only find solace in faith.

*

Tonia knelt devoutly on the leaf mould and prayed aloud for our sufferings to halt. But now and then praise for the British soldiers slipped out, for they had been forced to obey such bestial orders and we could only blame the incompetent politicians for directing such unchristian affliction upon us. After all it was the *Germans* who had uprooted *us* from our homes under the duress of SS guns and in such a violent way that even the most hard-hearted were shocked by Nazi crimes. Surely it was the German nation's duty to take care of those whom they had so wickedly uprooted from their homes and who had managed to survive the Nazi holocaust? But in those days we were in a tiny minority. Our voices were unheard – we had no television, or reporters to write in the national newspapers – and the politicians of the time sent over two million Cossacks to the Soviet Union to face death before their tormentors. What of those other millions whose deaths are not recorded?

*

Tonia and I were deeply preoccupied with our thoughts. The birds were chirping furiously, flying from one tree to the other: at times they fought over an insect then fled rapidly. The noise from the birds and the firing obscured the soldiers' footsteps. The woods suddenly began to crackle, then a moment later our safe place of hiding turned into hell.

The soldiers' hound-like yells increased in intensity as they trundled into position at the rear of the farmhouse. I heard a sharp yell, then the shuffling noise of a bayonet poking through the leaves.

'*Raus, raus!*' said the voices . . . How well we understood those words from our past.

Tonia's heart was racing in her chest: her lips turned dark blue and were trembling as we heard a gush of heavy footsteps from what seemed to be very burly men leaping straight at us. We clung to each other, too frightened to utter a word. Suddenly my legs seemed to die. One of the soldiers bawled in lurid rage, parting the undergrowth with his hands while his mate crushed it with his bayonet. Even as we cried, 'Oh Lord!' a third soldier caught hold of Tonia's legs. There was a sinister struggle: they grabbed us insanely – it was like a wrestling ring in the air – twisting and wrenching us from our nest. The soldiers' incoherent words were lost in the woodland echo.

Meanwhile, the overfed Austrian farmer who had betrayed us stood timidly by with a fixed stare. The soldier finally clutched me by my arm and we were carried off in the warm light back towards the bridge. I asked the soldier for water with which to wet my lips, but he reacted with a stream of unintelligible words. When I begged to be left in the woods the sterner and more unapproachable soldier replied only by pointing his rifle viciously at our heads. Although I could scarcely walk and kept falling down, we were pushed with the rifles always at our backs all the way across the bridge. Involuntarily, we followed the path which had been the scene of so much futile struggle and confusion.

On the other side of the bridge, my attention fell on a small hollow on the trampled grass where I saw the remains of the most frightful carnage of five people: a man had shot his wife and their three children before shooting himself. While his family lay facing the blue sky the man's body was all twisted, with his revolver beside him. Those were the bodies of Irina and Pyotr Mordovkin and their three children: their struggle for life had ended by the River Drau rather than at the hands of the Soviets. All their doubts and turmoil had been washed from their hearts. No harm could come to them now from the armed soldiers who guarded the bridge.

If only that bridge could talk of the tragedy it witnessed during those awful events. But only a spiritual – or even cursed – tale remained. After the tragedy, every fibre of the bridge was swept away by the strong waters. I believe that the Austrian authorities tried three times to rebuild the bridge, and three times it was swept away. In the end they had to give up.

*

As we neared the square with the soldiers, our feet shuffling along the ground, we trembled at the battered shambles which lay in our gaze. A large crowd still remained and Major Davies was talking to a group of priests. Pausing in his nervous walk, his eyes were stained with tears: he must have received some relevant information but, judging by his expression, whatever he had learned concerning the Forcible Repatriation was of no avail to us. I could not help but feel profoundly sorry for Major Davies, who had suddenly found himself in the centre of a political conflict and as a result was everlastingly disgraced in the eyes of the Good Lord.

The priests were raising blazes all over the camp. The British, therefore, were determined, come what may, to separate the priests from the rest, believing that once the leaders were out of the way, the remaining people might go without a struggle.

Everything in front of me was a jumble of harrowing revelations. I saw it all clearly, yet could not believe my eyes. The living were mixed up with the dead by the square. I could hear their raving and felt that they themselves had reached the brink of insanity. Brown patches of congealed blood surrounded the small body of a man who had been trampled to death. His two little girls tugged furiously at his arms – there was no sign of their Mama. All over the camp everyone looked as though they had been heavily sedated – in total confusion and disarray. Parents were searching for their children, alongside the heart-rending scene of whimpering orphans, like hundreds of little kittens, blindly looking for their own mamas and papas.

'By Heavens,' Tonia muttered. 'Why has the Good Lord deserted us?' She was grunting and gazed with inconsolable grief at a boy of about seven years old who had got hold of a soldier's hand as he shaded his eyes and was asking, 'Where is my Mama and Pa . . .?' Tears were falling off his cheeks. I did not hear the answer, but the soldiers marched the little boy away and placed him in a cattle wagon to wait for his Mama.

A dust-covered truck half-filled with tormented men, women and children, and with soldiers loosely holding their rifles at the front, stopped just behind us.

'Oh God, this is it,' Tonia screamed. The soldiers quickly mustered their strength and put their sins at a distance. Impatiently, the driver and some of the other soldiers hoisted Tonia, myself and a tattered ten-year-old girl up into the truck. A wretched chill of sweat came upon me as we were thrown amongst the old and the wounded, whose faces were contorted from the agony of cruelty. I stole a look at my companions, who were discussing our uncertain fate. Even at that point I did not believe the shameful uncertainty: I merely thought that we were heading to receive some medical treatment, since nearly all of us were wounded to different degrees. But neither our body wounds nor those in our hearts made any impression on the victorious soldiers. We were to be dragged to the slaughter on the orders of the merciless government, as though we were criminals.

The truck sped along the narrow dirt road to the spot where the cattle wagons were waiting, on a specially built wooden platform only a few hundred yards away from the main camp. Once the truck had backed up against one of the dirty cattle wagons, we were dragged out, a few at a time, and shoved into it. A deafening rumble of death cries emanated from the terror-stricken train. At this point, Tonia and I were separated when she was pushed into the furthest corner, while I landed on top of a grey-bearded man who was trying to mop up some of the blood from his hairless crown.

In the corner by the door was a small bucket for squatting into – no other luggage, or food, or water was in sight. When I looked deeper inside the death wagon, a streak of wildness came over me and I wriggled violently towards the open door. One thought stood out in the chaos of my brain: I was not going anywhere! As soon as the truck backed away, I dangled my legs over the exit.

A British medic, Dr John Pinching, was tending someone on the ground, the regret for what was happening clearly visible in his tearful eyes. He looked up, just before the door was bolted, and noticed my bleeding body and without a moment's hesitation simply pulled me off the death wagon. The next thing I knew I was hobbling along with several other wounded people to the first-aid tent near by. We had not gone very far when a soldier dashed towards us, yelling loudly and pointing to the wagons. The medic held me firmly by the arm and pointed to the bloody patches on my dress before giving the soldier a good raging. The soldier was obviously annoyed by the doctor's interference but he went away.

Over the years I have occasionally talked about those bitter events, but initially people thought that I was raving mad – the *British* would not do such things. It was twenty-nine years before I described Dr Pickering's gallant efforts to alleviate the sufferings of the victims – even when the lustre had faded from their eyes – to Lord Bethell for his book, *The Last Secret*. How well I remember my relief that at last the historical facts were to be published.

*

By the time the medic had patched up my wounds more trucks had arrived at the railway sidings. I fumbled desperately in my dress pocket for my Yugoslavian identity card. When I found it it was stained with blood, but still readable and I waved it at the medic. He understood what I was trying to tell him and placed me beside the non-Soviet nationalities. It was perhaps just as well that I did not know at the time how my false identity card could have led me into a similar fate to that which I had escaped. Many unfortunate Yugoslavs were also returned by force to their country, not only from the British zone but from American-occupied areas as well. In his book *Victims of Yalta* Count Tolstoy has well documented both the American and the British participation in the Forcible Repatriation.

I became involved in a mad scramble after the medic had left to look after the wounded who were to be taken to Lienz hospitals. One unsympathetic soldier caught hold of me by my shoulders and escorted me back to the cattle wagons. Clumsily, he twice let my body slip down between the wagon and the platform, before tossing me up into the air like a rag doll. As he pushed me inside the wagon, a sense of grief gnawed at my heart while I watched more and more reluctant victims jumping off the wagons, only to be caught again by the guard. It was useless to ask for help: no one could hear your voice amid the screams and firing guns.

I could see only Tonia's hand over in the corner of the wagon. The rest of her was trapped under the mass of bodies. The unimpressed soldiers were again trying to bolt the doors. A weak echo broke through the turmoil of my emotions. What am I to do? A firm voice in the back of my head rang out loud and clear, 'Jump, jump.'

The soldier outside was fidgeting with his rifle, aiming it roughly at the runaways, his mind clouded with anger and the illusion of triumph. I refused to endure any more cruelty and, disregarding the vindictive threats of the bullets, I jumped off the cattle wagon and ran with all my might to the Red Cross tent. Panting breathlessly, and sobbing, I waved my identity card in front of the medic and asked if I could stay there since I had nowhere to go in Russia. It was true, at the time I did not know if my parents were dead or alive.

Lt-Col Alec Malcolm who was supervising the loading, gave the final command to his soldiers to bolt all the cattle wagons with a metal bar. Can you imagine the unspeakable indignation of those inside, shut in without windows or fresh air?

After a long argument with the medic I was left behind, sitting in the tent. I will always be grateful to Dr Pinching for his intervention: without it I too would have perished by now in the Archipelago, with all the other millions of fugitives. For those who were not shot – as the great writer Alexander Solzhenitsyn has

personally witnessed while imprisoned himself in the Archipelago
— were all sent there, to destruction.

*

I hobbled alongside the Drau in the summer dusk, through the
shades of silence, hesitating to imagine the possible future of those
in the cattle wagons. No one was now allowed to cross the bridge,
but the wounded and other stragglers continued to sneak through
the woods on the other side. There were still a lot of soldiers all
along the dark stretches, with their row of guns: the dusk was filled
with red flashes illuminating the foliage below the mountains.

All that remained on the square were mutilated fragments of the
platform and patches of blood. The priests and the people had all
gone. Their small bundles of personal possessions were resting by
the barracks, but no one knew what to do with them or with the
remaining horses which roamed about the camp like black ants. A
scared child was sitting desolately, crying her heart out. I sat beside
her and patted her dark curly locks, but she kept saying, 'Mama,
where are you?' The remains of a rag doll lay by the little heap of
someone's belongings and a black flag ruffled in the breeze beside
it. A horse-driven cart stationed by the bridge was filled with the
dead.

I listened avidly to the bitter murmurs coming from the people
who were gathering the dead. I could hardly see, I was so shaken
by the spirit of sacrifice around me.

My own clothes were dishevelled and rustled about my body in
the wind. I was left in the wilderness – in a strange and unfriendly
world – all alone.

Night was falling and I looked for a place in which to sleep in
one of the few barracks that had escaped the damage. Over the
River Drau a tiny ray shone through the twilight. Humbly, I
accepted my refuge.

The daylight had faded, like my friends in the cattle wagons who
perished in the fierce claws of the infamous Archipelago. The scars
faded like roses, but the procession of faces and figures are
imbedded in my mind for ever. We were forced into this conflict of
war so suddenly – without a moment of peace in which to say
goodbye – but the memories of you all in my heart will never die.

CHAPTER SEVEN

NO PLACE AND NO HOME

I could not stay any longer in Peggetz Camp and so, without really knowing what I was going to do, I slipped away by myself and walked to the centre of Lienz. There I heard that a British transport would be departing shortly for Villach. They were transferring some refugees to the displacement camp there – and would take anyone else who wished to go.

I had no idea where Villach was but thought that anything would be better than staying at Peggetz, with the recent tragedy still so fresh in my mind. There were several British trucks sitting in the square, and I climbed into one which was already filled with all kinds of refugees who had been left behind from the Forcible Repatriation.

As the truck moved along the road, some of the older people tried to smile, or say something to try and make us laugh. But none of us could bring ourselves to laughter, or conversation, and the 115-kilometre journey passed mostly in silence. We did not even want to know anything about each other.

The camp at Villach, with its wooden barracks, was much the same as the one we had just left. Not only did it look the same, but we had hardly settled on our wooden bunks when the whispers began to travel round the barrack, saying that there was going to be the same process of Forcible Repatriation from this camp too! It was clear that Villach could not offer me the safety I was seeking.

I had become friendly with a young woman called Galya, who told me that she had heard about a huge camp in Weidmansdorf, about sixty kilometres away from Villach. It was said that it was more difficult for them to repatriate the refugees without their consent from there. I did not waste much time worrying about the details and decided to go right away. Galya needed no persuasion to come with me.

We managed to get a short lift at one stage, but by the time we reached Klagenfurt we had walked for the best part of the way. Eventually, we found Weidmansdorf, which was only about seven kilometres from Klagenfurt. The place was indeed huge, consisting of five separate compounds, each with its own mass of wooden barracks.

Weidmansdorf was only one of the many displacement camps which had sprung up all over Europe. It was bursting with refugees from every country – all violently bruised by the war. When I first arrived the difficult task of looking after the mass of people was in the hand of UNRRA (United Nations Refugee and Rehabilitation Association). I was to stay there for almost two years.

After a while, I began to work in the camp's Red Cross clinic, assisting the doctor and an Austrian nurse. In addition to helping with the patients' minor problems I was able to utilise my ear for languages by interpreting the Slavonic languages into German.

I must have been the busiest teenager in the camp. To preserve my alertness, I threw myself into a host of other activities: a nativity play, weekend dancing or swimming in Lake Maria Worth near by – anything to get away from the only topic of conversation in the camp, namely hunger. For as much as the administrators tried to alleviate our hunger, to stop our craving for exquisite dishes and all the things that we would have liked to have had, the sheer scale of our needs was too vast to cope with. The war may have ended, but the hopes we had cherished and, for myself, the single purpose for which I had survived, seemed as distant as they had ever been.

At the clinic where I worked there were many elderly people sitting, day after day, on the wooden bench: they were like statues, grey, emaciated and with hideous wounds on their bodies which never seemed to respond to treatment. They were long past any meaningful existence and could only find their comfort in prayer to God.

The realisation of my own grief came to me most deeply in darkness. I would lie in my bunk, crossing and uncrossing my arms a thousand times in a broken shallow sleep, trying to make sense of right and wrong, until even they had lost their meaning.

I can never understand the workings of God, especially when it comes to children: but then no one understands these things. We held a baby clinic every Monday, and often my heart almost split in two when I heard them crying on their empty stomachs. There was nothing for us to feed them with and their mothers' breasts dangled on their chests, empty. There was, however, one small consolation. Before each baby clinic, it was my duty to obtain from the camp store a small ration of dry milk and bars of chocolate for the very sick among them: the rest had to do without.

Scarcity of food was not the only problem we had to cope with. Shortly after the Forcible Repatriation at Peggetz, Austria was overrun with the Russian military. They paid particular attention to the displacement camps. At Weidmansdorf, the Soviets arrived frequently to interrogate everyone whom they felt might have some Russian connection, irrespective of their wishes. Thoughout the period in which UNRRA was looking after the camp the Soviets would come dressed in British uniforms. Later, however, when the camps had been taken over by the British Army, the Soviets still continued to come, but in their own uniforms – with chests full of medals. It was very frightening for me when I had to face four such men on one occasion. Yet again, it was my identity card, together with my ability to slip into other languages, which enabled me to escape the net.

As I was supposed to be Yugoslavian, I had an interpreter to translate the Soviets' questions from Russian into Yugoslavian. The time lapse between the original question and the translation directed at me gave me a few moments in which to collect my thoughts and reply in faultless Yugoslavian. I had already memorised the names of my fictitious family, the place where I came from and even the school I went to, with the help of a Yugoslavian family whom I had got to know.

I was one of the lucky ones. There were many who were not so lucky, unable to speak any other language and so deceive their interrogators: they had to go back to the Soviet Union. There were some, too, who would rather commit suicide than allow themselves to fall into the hands of the Soviets, and did so before their scheduled departures: the more able ones would disappear into the mountains, chancing their lives in a dangerous environment.

Gradually, the British became less willing to give their co-operation, and by the time I was ready to leave for Germany they would no longer allow the Soviets to harass the refugees whenever it could be avoided. They eventually posted civilian guards outside the camp gates.

*

A long time before I was born a certain handsome boy with flaxen hair was playing hockey at school in Canada. He was to become my husband, and with his help I have been able to build my new life on the wreck left by the past's evil events.

We met in Weidmansdorf by chance, after UNRRA had handed over the camp to the British Army. Arthur arrived with the rest of the British personnel, to take charge of the supplies.

It was November and the air was cold and grey. My little iron stove had gone cold and there was no more wood to burn, so when my duty relief came at 9.30 pm I went to the dance hall to keep warm.

My heart began to thump when I saw a tall, blond sergeant, handsome in his British uniform, coming towards me. As we danced to the tune *Jealousy* his cheek came close to mine: I felt myself smiling in response to his gentleness. We soon became firm friends, but I never told him anything about my past life in the Nazi camps or about the freshly wounding episode of the 'Forcible Repatriation' of the Russians from Lienz. Our worlds were miles apart.

But however disparate our occupations and personal status, there was certainly no division between us on one point: love. Six months later we were engaged.

What a splendid party it turned out to be! The room where Arthur stayed at the nearby Austrian guesthouse, and the long corridor leading up to it, were filled with flowers, gifts of crystal, many mementoes, even an enormous cake with all the trimmings, carnival cakes and candies. There was a special gift, too, from the children's clinic which they had made themselves: a tiny paper heart covered with kisses. I was overcome with the most moving and unforgettable feeling. I remembered many parties and festivals back home, always splendid and full of tradition but rather boring for a child, but *this* was a spontaneous act of love and flowers.

After the celebration had ended, we talked together about Arthur's boyhood in Canada and his military service in Britain and discussed at length the possibility of our eventually being able to live permanently in Britain or maybe Canada. I was not very sure what to do as I had still not been in contact with my parents since I was taken away in 1943.

Although I knew that I could not return, even to visit them, in the foreseeable future, perhaps the situation would change. I refused to give up hope. But *Canada* seemed so far away from my home; if we were going to live anywhere then it would have to be Britain. It was a big step to take.

One day, Arthur discussed my problem with one of the Red

Cross representatives, and through him we were able to send my two personal letters off to Russia. Unknown to me, Mama had already held a memorial service for me after she heard no word from me once the war had ended. I waited patiently, every day for a scrap of news from home, but all in vain.

Meanwhile, the Red Cross had informed the camp official that Britain required a number of young people to work in the cotton mills, jute mills and coal mines. The would-be candidates were to be vetted first by the Control Commission in Germany, where the authorities were still looking for the Nazi war criminals who were masquerading among the genuine refugees.

I had set my heart on continuing to work in a hospital. Since the British required only factory workers, there seemed little or no chance of me being accepted for such work: nevertheless, I filled in the appropriate form with my particular request for a hospital position in Scotland. I remember the Red Cross lady glancing over my form with a smile, before warning me, 'The British government's wheels are grinding rather slowly nowadays. You may have to wait a year for a reply!'

There was no rush, I told her. I had nothing much to ship over: all I had was one pale-pink dress and a pair of wine-coloured shoes obtained from the Red Cross depot and which could only be replaced when they had worn out. I received no pay for working each day at the clinic. Instead, I was given an extra ration of soup from the camp kitchen! I did not need a lot of clothes, however, because I was always in my uniform: a blue-and-white striped dress, white apron and the white cap with a red cross in the centre which hid most of my hair. The outfit was pretty and smart, and the envy of all who saw it!

Often the doctor would take me with him to bandage someone and help him calm the atmosphere during the turbulent brawl which often erupted. On one occasion we were called to a battle between some Turkish and Yugoslavian refugees. They had drunk themselves into an uncontrollable frenzy and many of them had revolvers, knives, broken bottles – one even had a scythe! There we were in the middle of this crowd, covered in blood, and armed only with syringes and bandages!

The barrack smelt like dung. The carousing had reached its climax at the top of the long wooden table. It was no use attempting to have a direct conversation with their leader when more toasts were still being drunk to the health of everybody who

147

fought against the Nazi machine: the King of Britain, Winston Churchill and the whole of America! I was really scared . . . and yet I felt peculiarly sad to watch these drunken men, defeated not merely on the surface, but in their souls.

*

The winter was now behind us and the sweet Spring of hope appeared in subtle warmth. I could not help but be deeply worried about my fate. Being a 'Yalta Victim' and trapped like a fly in a spider's web, my health had definitely suffered. The large blisters I got on my feet as a result of walking from Lienz to Klagenfurt had obstinately refused to heal. I should have been happy to be alive — even though I was living in a little hole like a rabbit. But I could not return home under Stalin's regime: there was only one destiny for people like me, however innocent — and that was death.

However, I knew I could not stay in the camp for ever and had no idea when I would hear from Britain. There had not been a more desperate moment than then and a more pressing need of Mama's comforting arms around me, to ease the pain in my heart.

Some say that it is God's will to suffer. But I cannot argue with God — if I could, then, I would gladly have given up my young life for the peace and freedom of the world.

Survival was hard. Some of the refugees at the camp, particularly those who were educated Tsarists, or the Kulaks, showed much indolence in their attitude and did not want to bother with any camp work as they believed that they were above it all. But I worked like a slave from six thirty in the morning when I would roll up my sleeves, scrub the floor, make my bed and light the iron stove in my tiny barrack room, providing there was any wood left. I would check that my uniform was spotless and only then was I ready to start the full day's work.

At seven thirty one morning I was eating my butterless slice of bread when I heard a gentle tap on the door. I knew that it must have been something very special when I found Arthur standing in the doorway giving nothing away about his secret. He paused for a moment, rubbing his hands together.

'My darling, your permit for Britain is now in the main office. You must be very privileged to get it so quickly, precisely within three weeks!'

I remember listening intently and, with much emotion, fell into

Arthur's arms. The little happiness that we had was now at an end.
A parting time again. Who knows? We might never see each other
again.

We talked for a while. He seemed such a clear-sighted and
earnest man, never failing to find something kind to say. He tried
to reassure me that our parting would be very brief, only until his
army career came to an end in a year's time. However convincing
our talk may have been, I had *other* thoughts on my mind.

That evening we danced to the soft background music: *Until
Then My Darling Please Wait for Me* seemed most appropriate for
two young people madly in love. There were lots of tears and
kisses until the early hours of the morning.

*

Two days later I was on my way to Germany in transport fit only
for pigs. On the morning when we were taken to the railway
station it came as a dreadful shock to see the familiar sight of cattle
trucks staring me in the face. Even though the war had ended we
still seemed to be treated worse than animals. It reminded me at
once of my journey from Russia, only this time the sliding doors
had been left unbolted and there was fresh straw in one corner.

It was one of the longest trains I had ever seen. What a long time
it took to fill the cattle trucks: people were saying their goodbyes,
in some cases perhaps for ever. Galya had seen this type of
transport before and refused to come with me to the station,
knowing that one day she also must leave Austria in the same
disappointing way.

It was late afternoon before we set off. I kept trying to look at
the picturesque countryside, but could not really concentrate on its
beauty, already regretting having chosen this path but knowing
that it was too late to change my mind.

I thought of all the wonderfully friendly people that I had left in
Weidmansdorf. Who, I wondered, would be helping Dr Ivanovich
with the children's clinic now? And how was I going to keep my
promise to stay in touch with the Ostashkievich family? They had
been so kind and loving and treated me as one of their own
children: their son Ivan was my own age and Vera, their daughter,
was a few years older. I never did manage to keep in touch with
them: by the time I got a permanent address I heard that they had
emigrated to Venezuela. I wonder where they are now?

We were supposed to be going to Britain, but nobody knew our next destination. All day, then all night the train kept moving, often at no more than a crawling pace. I could not sleep, so I watched the dawn come up, bringing a sparkling sunny morning.

Our train came to a halt at one station, but we could hardly get out to stretch our legs as the platform was so devastated: rubble from the buildings and railway tracks was piled up in the air. No one knew which town or station it was, as there were no signposts. How long we took after this stop, I cannot say – I slept for the rest of the journey, only waking when the British trucks arrived to take us from the final station to Delmenhorst.

*

Delmenhorst transit camp was as wild as hell – huge, bleak and surrounded by swamps. Here again I met all sorts of different nationalities: Hungarians, French, Russians, Latvians, Yugoslavians. I even met some Belgians. We were taken to a large hall with a pile of mattresses in one corner and smelling strongly of carbolic. Every night we had to lay out the mattresses on the floor before we could go to sleep and in the morning we would lift them up and put them back against the wall, while the floor was washed with carbolic.

It was one of the worst camps I have ever stayed in. Everything was chaotic. No one knew where anything was: the civilian in charge of our barrack knew even less. The only meal of the day was some kind of stew served on a plate.

It was while I was standing in a long queue to receive my meal that I overheard a Ukrainian family talking about how the American and the British governments had agreed to send back all the Russians and Ukrainians to the Soviet Union. They, it seemed, had avoided the repatriation by changing their nationality to Polish. But it did not matter to me any more and I did not attempt to talk to them.

Thankfully, I did not have to stay at Delmenhorst for very long. The following week I was called for my medical examination. I had to show the doctor my displaced person's card: he merely wrote down my number and after sounding my chest, with a quick glance at my eyes, I was allowed to return to the camp. Many other people were not so fortunate. Some had tuberculosis or other terminal diseases and as no country was willing to accept them, they were sent to the various hospitals in Hamelin.

One week after our medical, a group of about five hundred of us were called to a strange, kidney-shaped room. It had a high counter with glass windows above it, running from one end of the room to the other. No one told us why we were there, and it was very frightening to say the least. We had to walk slowly round the room, and with each step I took, there was a different face staring at me from the other side. How was I to know that this was the British Control Commission I had heard about, and that they were looking for Nazi war criminals?

Two days later, we saw that many British trucks had arrived in the camp, and only then were we told to prepare at once for our departure. There was not really very much preparation to be done: most of the young refugees had no luggage, except for one older woman of twenty-two. I remember her saying that she was Hungarian, but she looked more like a German spy to me, with her ginger-blonde hair slightly hidden under a beautifully tailored blue hat, surrounded by all her suitcases.

They were British drivers, two to each truck. The trucks did not stop until we reached Bremerhaven. On the clear blue waters a huge white ship was staring at us in the sunshine.

*

A mixed crowd of passengers were on the top deck: military police, soldiers returning home on leave and the many families, who took up most of the ship. The only available space for the refugees was in the engine room where the noise was deafening.

I was given a hammock when I arrived, but as soon as the ship began to move over the rough waters I became so seasick that I had to be moved to a wooden bunk so that the ship's attendant could keep an eye on me. On our second day at sea I was still sick. The whole place was spotlessly clean, but the kindly attendant came to change my bed linen and insisted that I had to try and eat something in the dining-room along with everyone else. She thought that the change would make me feel better.

Although I felt very weak I managed to dress and slowly went up the stairs with the attendant by my side. The tables in the dining-room were packed with those people who were lucky enough to be unaffected by sea-sickness. All the tables were covered with gleaming white tablecloths, with silver cutlery and beautiful crockery. I had not seen anything like it since I left home.

I settled down to enjoy myself – everything was most charming and I was so looking forward to the pleasure of some tasty food in such splendour. But as soon as the steward put a small plate of white fish in front of me I felt sick again and could not eat a thing.

The next thing I remember we were at Tilbury Docks.

The smart uniforms of the 'green ladies' (WVS) stood out in sharp contrast to the drab refugees on the quayside. They were there to escort us to our final refugee camp at Wigesly, near Lincoln. I never saw them again, or any other relief organisation for that matter. I was all alone and still a teenager – in my new country in the free West. Suddenly, a new horizon was opening up, revealing a surprisingly strange world.

Britain looked to be a wonderful country: on my way to King's Cross station with the 'green ladies' I admired the different styles of the ancient and impressive buildings. I saw too, with great sadness, much devastation in the city. London had been bombed so savagely by the Germans that there were many streets which consisted of nothing more than crushed rubble. Yet the people in the streets were all well dressed and jubilantly happy. They were very brave.

It was not surprising to me that they were so pleased with themselves, in spite of the lingering war and the hardship they had endured. They had not known the terror of occupation; their heroism had not yielded to the Nazi attacks and they had kept Hitler away from their country. My world would have been so different if Stalin's Red Army had not abandoned his civilians to the Nazis' claws.

I shall always remember too the dream-like quality of Lincoln city, with its honey-coloured towers rising majestically above the mediaeval buildings, the swans gliding down the blue water which reflected their shadows beneath them. It was sheer tranquillity after Delmenhorst.

*

Many years later, when I got in touch with the United Nations High Commissioner for Refugees to ask for some form of restitution, they evaluated my sufferings at the sum of 940 dollars, *on condition* that I provide them with positive proof that I had been in Auschwitz. As I still cannot remember the exact date I was first taken to the camp (I wonder would many children remember under such stress?) and the Russian children were not tattooed at the time and did not receive any passports in Auschwitz, I could not comply with this impossible request. In the end, the United Nations declined any form of restitution, even though they knew by that time that the Soviet government had positively identified me as their citizen and offered me a passport.

The public tend to respond wholeheartedly when the word 'refugee' is used, but somehow in this modern world our priorities have gone astray, and compassion is masked by sickening bureaucracy. My claim had to be abandoned and I never got any help from the United Nations, or from anyone else.

Forty years later, the world is still full of refugees.

CHAPTER EIGHT

MOSCOW PROMISE

How can I ever describe my feelings that morning as the taxi sped along the Moscow streets. My unsophisticated mind was bursting with unanswerable questions. We flashed by the modern shops and buildings and the astonishing window displays of pretty dresses and typical Muscovite outfits caught my eye. This part of Moscow was completely unknown to us. At one point, a large convoy of trucks full of hay appeared in the blinding sun, leaving behind them a floating grey dust which blurred the ugly multi-storey buildings.

But I had other things on my mind. I could not begin to express my excitement to the taxi driver: he would not understand it, though he looked old enough to have been involved himself in the Second World War. Instead, I asked him if he knew of any good opera in the city and we talked about Tolstoy's *Yasnaya Polyana*. He told me that all Tolstoy's books, furniture and paintings had been sent to Siberia for safety just before the German invasion, but that now everything had been restored to his original house and transformed into a museum. I was beginning to relax and enjoy our conversation, but as soon as Mr Gold mentioned the word 'football' my part in the dialogue ended abruptly. If there is one subject the Russians like to talk about, after food perhaps, then it must be football!

I had time to think; and a strange, unwelcome feeling started to fill my whole body – suddenly, I was afraid. In one way I was bitter that this should be the case: to feel frightened of Russian people, whose way of life I had shared from my birth to my schooldays. Was it only last night that we had been laughing and joking with the Russians in the restaurant, enthusiastically applauding the orchestra perched on its splendid stand? Everything then had been just perfect. I adored dancing to any tunes – tangos and foxtrots – and we had all danced very well, I thought. But now . . . life seemed so much more dramatic.

The taxi drew up in the forecourt of a large hotel. I could already see a tall man by the lamp-post. His face was partly hidden by dark glasses and, despite it being a warm, sunny morning, he wore a brown hat and navy blue raincoat. In fact, he could have been the twin brother of my more familiar 'companion'. He must have been most uncomfortable in the heat!

Mr Gold had also seen him. 'There he is,' he said, 'with the typical look of a Chicago gangster. Did I hear you say he is not a KGB agent? His KGB approach is sticking out a mile!'

He started to get out of the taxi, but then he turned and, looking straight in to my eyes, suggested that it would be wiser if I stayed in the taxi while he went over to speak to the man. Seconds later, he changed his mind: 'How the hell could I speak to him in Russian – I don't know a word of the language. You'd better come too, but please instruct the taxi driver to wait.'

I was lost in admiration, for I knew that none of this would have been possible if Mr Gold had decided to stay a little longer in his bed! We learned straight away that his initial suspicions had been right: the man in dark glasses *was* a KGB agent. He had shadowed Mama all the way to Moscow and traced me to my hotel. I said nothing and the two men could only communicate in sign language, but it was enough to find out that Mama was waiting patiently for me in one of the hotel rooms.

While we were following the KGB man along the labyrinth of mirrored corridors and passages Mr Gold stopped and looked back at me, as if he doubted the wisdom of our taking such risks.

'You had better memorise which way we are going, just in case you have to run back should this be a political trick.' He spoke slowly and thoughtfully: 'I'll look into the room first, and if your Mama is not there you must run as fast as you can and wait for me in the taxi.'

The door opened. I saw a lonely white-headed lady standing in front of me, smiling. Her wrinkled face expressed years of sorrow; the pale blue eyes were much paler than when I last looked into them, from all the tears they had shed. But I could feel the warmth of her emotions, even from a distance. After eighteen long years of turmoil there I was at last – in my Mama's caressing arms.

She fainted almost straight away. I brought her out of the faint with some smelling salts which I always carried in my handbag. Then I asked the gentlemen to leave the room so that Mama and I could talk in private. The KGB man was most reluctant to leave us and had to be literally ushered out by Mr Gold.

I could feel the passion of Mama's love and found myself responding as everyone should to a mother's love. We stood for a while, just looking at each other. She had not recognised her daughter. And then she spoke: 'My dearest little one – you have come back!'

Mama took me over to a long wardrobe mirror and stood beside me, embracing me. In barely a whisper she asked, 'Now let me see the old scar at the back of your neck! Do you remember how you got it?'

'Oh yes, I do indeed! You mean when I was climbing the old pussy-willows by the river and a dead branch broke – and I went down with it into the water, head first on a sharp stump!'

We were still overcome by our emotions – understandably so – when the KGB man came back to the room and suggested that we should all go down to share a champagne breakfast. I could not help feeling a bit suspicious, but we accompanied him down to the huge dining room.

My boss was already sitting with some other Russians at a table with a beautiful bouquet of flowers. We all celebrated Mama's belated, and most unforgettable, birthday. One of the men sitting near by, an agronomist, was taking a lot of interest in us. He was an older man with a fair complexion: he looked overfed and his podgy hands showed little evidence of hard work. But he had an educated mind and, after a few glasses of champagne, he began to put some of his arguments into English. As, again, is often the case in the Soviet Union, the topic of conversation was the Second World War.

He blamed Jewish greed for all the Nazis' atrocities. I did not pay much attention to that kind of talk, but I did sit up when he said, 'You don't own anything in the West – only the Jews do. They own all the banks, building societies, shops and factories and you sweat all the week for a few pounds to keep your soul together. The Jews will pay again with their blood for their greed.'

He had nearly come to blows with Mr Gold, who was bitterly defending the Jewish race, before the KGB man broke up the party. But before that superfluous heated talk was finally over, the agronomist snapped, 'The Jews are like the fascists – grabbing everything for themselves. They never help any other race – only their own kind.'

I retorted that this was surely not true, because I *saw* their suffering – and some kindness – in the camps. But, he never heard me.

We returned to our own hotel shortly after breakfast, promising to come back as soon as I had finished work.

*

That afternoon at the exhibition, I could not stop smiling in wonder at the fulfilment of my dream. I had to pinch my flesh to remind myself that my incredible happiness was real and that I had not been drawn into a whirlpool of fantasies.

That same evening, when the clock on the wall showed several minutes past seven, we left by taxi to go again to the Kievskaya hotel. We drove for an hour and made endless diversions from one street to another so that we could see as much of Moscow as possible. Nevertheless, when we arrived, my 'own' KGB agent from the exhibition was already walking casually by the hotel.

I did not feel hungry and so Mr Gold went to dine by himself, while I went straight to Mama's room. When I arrived, the man from the KGB was talking to Mama in the strangest manner, whereas a sense that her heart was breaking made it impossible for her to speak. It was as though he was lecturing to some political class. Impulsively he walked towards me and asked, 'What do you say, Zoe?'

'I really have not a great deal to say to strangers like you,' I replied, on the defensive. My heart felt the terror of interrogation as his eyes scanned every inch of my body.

'Tell me briefly,' he said, 'about your young upbringing within the western capitalist materialism.'

'I was too busy trying to repair my own broken life, so there was no time to notice anything else,' I said brightly, staring uncertainly at the ceiling. He took notes, snapped shut his briefcase and then poured himself a glass of tea from the boiling samovar. He swallowed his tea so quickly that he burned his tongue, but even that could not deter him from talking about, as he put it, 'the cancerous, unjust western capitalist society which is still shackled with ideological tactics in human exploitation'.

Memories of the Soviets' injustice towards their own people during the Forcible Repatriation and of how many of those people were murdered the moment they reached Soviet soil troubled my mind. I felt an inner urge to tell him to go to the devil, but at that moment I thought it would only mean the end of me and my freedom – and worse than that, no one would ever know what had happened to us. Normally, no one could argue or even reason with the KGB. Their word was law. But I continued to challenge him on every point. Waves of irritability rippled on his face and I expected him to explode any moment, but it came to nothing: he merely leaned against the wall. Mr Gold came to my rescue just in time. When I look back I realise that he really was a marvel. He persuaded the KGB man to accompany him to the bar: the longer he was safely drinking whisky, the longer Mama and I would have to talk without his intrusion.

The glare of the evening was almost finished. Mama's rheumatic hands were a blur in the dim light: I felt her shivering cheeks against mine. At once she asked me to write about the frightful journey of a scared and lonely thirteen-year-old girl across Europe from Russia.

We were leaning out of the window with our heads outside, so that our conversation could not be recorded on the microphone which was concealed in the central light. Mama continued, 'We too suffered from the cold winters, and our food was in short supply for the amount of work we had to do. But you were the purpose of my life – *your* life was enough to distract me from these hardships. No one knows how it feels to have a child and not be allowed to see her. But with the acknowledgement of my grief here is a tranquillity which I have never in my life experienced until now.'

Mama also told me how she had read about the large British Trade Fair which was to be held in Moscow. She had determined there and then to travel to the capital, with the hope that she might find me there. She had not received my letters, but had been driven by the same blind hope and trust in fate which had brought me from my home. When and where the KGB had caught up with her, I am not sure. I only know that he had travelled all the way from Odessa Region. His motives were immaterial to us: we had managed to find each other and that was all that mattered.

The shadow of the man who had followed me from the exhibition filtered below the hotel window; the sound of his feet in the cold night appeared to penetrate the quietness of our room. A few birds were still awake and strutted on the ridges of the roof. Mama pointed silently at the man. I could see clearly that his right hand was firmly placed on the gun in his pocket. It could easily have been fired by mistake: no one could ever be sure in the dusk.

He watched us closely with curiosity and shrewdness. It was like being involved in a James Bond film – only the drama was really happening to me!

We remained for some time in the cool breeze from the open window and poured out our hearts to each other, reliving the faded nightmare years in slow motion. At times, our words blurred into profound whispers and with a sense of exultation we cleansed our minds of the past's evil events. There was so much to talk about that I hardly knew where to start and with each incident I recalled, a dull pain throbbed at the base of my subconscious.

A sharp image of the faces of old people and children came back to me — faces in a train. Often there was someone I seemed to recognise, but whose right name I could not remember. With the added stress of the KGB outside, I could hardly think. It reminded me of the visit I had from them in Scotland and I told Mama all about it.

'You are a very brave little girl,' Mama said, while wiping the tears from her cheeks. She took a deep breath, as though she wanted to put aside all her crying, before telling me about my friend Tonia, who had returned to the Soviet Union after the Forcible Repatriation only to stand trial. After the trial, Mama told me, she had been sent away to one of the labour camps which have been so vividly described by Alexander Solzhenitsyn, and no one has ever heard from her since.

In his book, *The Gulag Archipelago*, Solzhenitsyn used the real names of the people he encountered, with total disregard to their living relatives who could have suffered as a repercussion. I myself was later to learn how real a danger this was when I innocently divulged my own account of what happened during the Forcible Repatriation to the Soviet Union to Lord Bethell, for his book, *The Last Secret*. I did not disguise my name and shortly after the publication of his book, the resulting documentary *Orders from Above* and other public controversies in the British media, my only brother was punished with his life.

I received the saddest telegram from the Soviet Union containing the most harrowing words. It read: 'Your brother has died. Come to the funeral.' No matter how often I enquired about the nature of his illness, to this day, his sudden death is still shrouded in mystery.

I did not attend the funeral and was only glad that, by that time, Mama was already dead and spared that further episode in our years of turmoil.

*

Four days later, in the warm glow of the evening, Mr Gold and I arrived at the Kievskaya hotel to say goodbye to my Mama. It had been the shortest – and happiest – four days I had ever known and this was the last evening that I was to spend with Mama.

Even with Mr Gold by my side I felt most unsafe: we were under the watchful eye of the KGB and I could never be sure whether it was really meant for my own safety. Mr Gold disliked any parting, and so he said his respectful farewell to Mama before hurrying downstairs to the bar with the KGB man, leaving Mama and myself alone once more.

That evening, the light in the room was dim. Mama was standing by the open window, a frail little lady who had retained so much of her love, warmth and dignity, without ever complaining. She was small, but had a big generous heart; she had given me my life at the cost of much sorrow to herself.

For some time she held much of the conversation, talking about everything which came into her mind so that she would not forget any of the things she wanted to tell me. It was as though she sensed that we would never meet again.

In turn, I tried to tell her that I would somehow get her a visa to enable her to come for a holiday in Scotland. Of course, at the time I was still very naïve about the difficulties faced by ordinary Soviet citizens who wished to travel to the West. I never was to succeed in bringing her to visit us.

As Mama put her arms around me, our hearts were about to be divided for ever. We both sensed it, but this feeling was left unexpressed, in silence. One part of me longed to go with Mama, but she said, 'Your place is now with Arthur. Be happy, my little one.'

I closed the door behind me and could hear Mama's hurtful sobs all the way along the dim-lit corridor. I never saw her again.

EPILOGUE

The year 1961 had brought me much joy at having fulfilled my promise to Mama. But when I learned that my friends were either dead or dying in Archipelago – without even knowing the kind of life and freedom that I had lived in the Western world – I felt sick at heart. Had I been a really good interpreter or a newspaper correspondent that would have given me the chance to expose the evil life and the lamentations behind the barbed wire in the Soviet Gulags. I did speak with many people about the wretched life which the betrayed prisoners had in the Soviet hands, but, there again, no one believed me.

I have even written to the United Nations, but their complacency and selfishness in their attitude towards this human deprivation has shaken my faith. Their failure to reply bewildered me. My letter to them may not have won a Nobel prize, but it was clear enough to alert the world and save a few lives.

Although they did not acknowledge my letter, I knew that they had received it because the following Christmas they had the audacity to write asking me for a generous donation. One day, during the United Nations collection, I asked the collector if he knew what it meant to him? Did he know, for example, who would benefit from the money he was collecting? Incredibly, he merely shook his head. Schoolchildren are often sent out on the streets and on door-to-door collections without any awareness that they are being used to help to keep the bureaucrats in the luxurious life-style to which they have become accustomed. The role of the United Nations in helping children is, in my eyes, a notorious earthly sin.

The fundamental principles of the British people, on the other hand, have touched me very deeply. I shall never forget one of the most moving moments in my life: when Lord Bethell telephoned and invited me to unveil the 'Yalta Victims Memorial' on 6 March 1982. I felt most humble that I had been given such a great honour and much relieved that the millions of victims who had suffered and perished in Soviet hands, were, at last, remembered in my new and unknown land of Britain.

At the ceremony, there were many kind and eminent people

and I had hoped that I would not weep, but as the choir of the Russian Orthodox Church in Exile began to sing under the cloudless sky the whole sorrowful scene of Peggetz came vividly before my tearful eyes.

Judge eternal, throned in splendour,
Lord of Lords and Kings of Kings,
With thy living fire of judgment
Purge this realm of bitter things:
Solace all its wide dominion
With the healing of thy wings.

Still the weary folk are pining
For the hour that brings release:
And the city's crowning clangour
Cries aloud for sin to cease;
And the homestead and the woodlands
Plead in silence for their peace.

*

Crown, O God, thine own endeavour:
Cleave our darkness with thy sword:
Feed the faint and hungry heathen
With the richness of thy Word:
Cleanse the body of this empire
Through the glory of the Lord.

*

I wept in silence.

Prime Minister Margaret Thatcher's compassion was enormously appreciated by my people when she contributed her help in obtaining the land in Thurloe Square where the Memorial now stands.

In my tiny way of gratitude, on 10 September 1982, I travelled with my husband to London, carrying one four-foot tall beautiful blue spruce and some Queen Elizabeth and Elizabeth of Glamis roses. With the kind permission of the London parks authority, these were planted in the mystic place of the 'Yalta Victims Memorial' gardens – to mark a little happiness to all who visit and rest there in tranquillity.